Reinventing the Garden

Chaumont – Global Inspirations from the Loire

Thames & Hudson

Louisa Jones

Reinventing the Garden

Chaumont – Global Inspirations from the Loire

With 238 illustrations, 229 in color

*To all those who keep the world
in touch with the earth.*

contents

First published in hardcover in the
United States of America in 2003 by
Thames & Hudson Inc., 500 Fifth Avenue,
New York, New York 10110

thamesandhudsonusa.com

Library of Congress Catalog Card Number
2003100801
ISBN 0-500-51133-0

Printed and bound in China
by C&C

The Chaumont Garden Festival is in its eleventh year…

In the beginning, I was not betting on the future. Fifteen years of organizing complicated exhibitions at a frantic pace for the Pompidou Centre had exhausted my enthusiasm. Gardening for a while seemed like a good idea. Getting out of Paris seemed like a good idea. Assuming it was only temporary…

Eleven years later, you can see the result.

Of course, other people's enthusiasm fed the fire in the meantime: Jack Lang, Minister of Culture at the time, made it all happen; the Centre region of France, faithful from the start, contributed much; the Conseil Général of the Loir-et-Cher department, could always be depended upon.

Not to mention private sponsors, so numerous that they cannot be listed here.

Why this interest in a garden festival? No doubt because gardening is not such an innocent and futile activity as it first seems. Gardens hold up a mirror to society: we are much more prosperous than fifty years ago, hence we grow flowers more than vegetables; we now travel a lot and hence our gardens are 'improved' with the inevitable stone sculptures, gourds and other exotic items that we cannot do without.

Instead of being merely an isolated event, the Garden Festival of Chaumont-sur-Loire was viewed from its first year as a pioneer outpost in garden design. From 1992 onwards, the great names of landscape architecture have wanted to participate; at the same time neophytes, today in the majority (for we attach great importance to this 'hand up' for the young) constantly bring in new blood.

In short, everyone works hard and has a good time. If we allow complete freedom for creative talents, we vigorously defend certain moral principles: finding examples from the past to build on for the future; making full use of new technologies and materials to the point of exploiting them in unexpected and playful ways; giving full sway to new plants and the promotion of botanic diversity; and above all, having a sense of humour, not taking ourselves too seriously, because gardening must always be a pleasure.

Obviously, most of us involved in this adventure avoid too much intellectualizing, building theoretical castles in the air…

Louisa Jones's book has come at just the right time to help us see clearly where we are. Her insatiable curiosity has brought to light many details that we had missed; her comparisons between gardens have delighted, surprised but never shocked us. In the beginning, Louisa had imagined that we would work together on this book. We preferred to discover an independent point of view and have no regrets. Her vision will captivate readers even as it helps us move into the future.

Jean-Paul Pigeat Chaumont, June 2002

I remember so well the day Jean-Paul Pigeat first contacted me to ask if I would be interested in participating in the first year of the Garden Festival of Chaumont-sur-Loire. More than a decade later I can still recall that time with the same emotion. This was my first project outside of Spain. A young gardener of 35, I was being offered the opportunity to become acquainted with and admire the work of artists I already esteemed highly. And above all, the most important thing, a chance to participate myself in the creation of gardens on this site and to share in the strong enthusiasm of this gardening world. I felt like a younger brother invited to discover the secrets of the masters. Never will I forget how Jacques Wirtz spoke to me when we first met at Chaumont, nor what I owe to him and also to all the other artists who participated in that inaugural year. All these exchanges remain fixed like stars in my spiritual firmament. I keep images of this 'voyage' that will never fade: the sinuous bamboo tunnel of Hiroshi Teshigahara, the elegant teak bench set simply in a parterre of white cosmos by Mark Rudkin, the mysterious grotto of Emilio Ambasz, the serpentine paths that linked each garden like a leaf to a branch in the ground plan of that master of subtlety, Jacques Wirtz. The Festival of Chaumont has brought together in the years of its brief existence so much beauty and emotion, ideas and enthusiasm, that it will always be a privilege for all of us to have participated, and to participate in future, in these exchanges which owe so much to the intelligence, tenacity and unshakable passion for gardens of Jean-Paul Pigeat.

I was happy to learn that a book would now be devoted to the study of Chaumont's varied achievements, written by an author whose work I have much admired in years past, Louisa Jones. Her blending of intelligent analysis with ardent enthusiasm is always worth reading.

Fernando Caruncho   October 2002

Translated from the Spanish by Bernard Dupont

introduction:
the chaumont story

The International Garden Festival of Chaumont-sur-Loire first opened its doors in 1992 and was already, in its first year, a showcase for innovative design. It has continued to attract leading names in landscape architecture and related fields: among the Americans, George Hargreaves, Peter Walker, Lynden B. Miller, Susan Child, Mark Rudkin and Andy Cao; among the Japanese Shodo Suzuki, Haruto Kobayashi, and Hiroshi Teshigahara; the Spaniard Fernando Caruncho, Hungarian Vladimir Sitta now based in Australia, and Dutch Adriaan Geuze. Famous French names include: Michel Desvigne and Christine Dalnoky, Louis Benech, Laure Quoniam, Jacques Simon, and Edouard François. Some members of the original 'home team', Eric Ossart and Patrick Blanc, have achieved international recognition in their own right after beginning their careers at Chaumont. At the same time, the Festival has realized its ambition to teach and form young talent, working with top design schools such as Kew, Harvard, Cornell, Genoa, Munich, Reggio Calabria and the Quasar Institute in Rome, to cite only the ones outside France.[1]

Chaumont is no longer merely an observation post of current trends, but an active participant in their creation. The *mosaïculture* or carpet bedding theme of 2001, dismissed as pure kistch by garden snobs, not only acknowledged the growing fascination among designers for plant sculpture but has helped make it acceptable to the general public. In May 2002 the trendy British magazine *Gardens Illustrated* offered an article on carpet bedding which noted Chaumont's choice approvingly in terms that aptly describe the Festival's function today: 'Here the method was freed of its historic associations and used to produce a range of exciting contemporary gardens. Perhaps, at last, this will put an end to a hundred years of the jokey image of carpet bedding, and it can be seen for what it is – a tool, waiting to be used by any gardener where enthusiasm and resources allow'.[2] Chaumont's founder, Jean-Paul Pigeat, once wrote: 'Always the same method... to use whatever is handy and normally just taken for granted to create something entirely new.'[3] The American landscape architect Peter Walker commented in 2002: 'I have been back four or five times and I have enjoyed the various gardens and even the failed attempts interest me very much.'

Nor has this been an adventure reserved for specialists: from the 60,000 visitors who came in 1992, Festival attendance grew to attain 163,000 in 2001. The season has expanded from two months in late summer to five, between June and October, each year organized around a different theme. The best proof of success lies perhaps in the proliferation of other garden festivals that cite Chaumont as an inspiration, most recently Westonbirt in Britain. Like Chaumont, any new festival requires imagination, backers, a place, a plan, a procedure, exhibitors and basic service facilities to ensure success. Above all, it needs ways to earn and keep the interest of a many-faceted, ever better informed public.

A One-Man Show

The Chaumont Festival is the brainchild of one man, Jean-Paul Pigeat. Born in Montluçon in 1946, Pigeat studied law and business before becoming a journalist specializing in environmental issues. In 1970 he published with Catherine Dreyfus *Les Maladies de l'environnement* (Diseases of the Environment), the first book in France to address problems such as chemical and noise pollution, rural disenchantment and mismanagement of France's architectural heritage. The same year, Pigeat began working with the O.R.T.F. (French national television) and produced several documentaries, including one on the French utopian visionary Charles Fourier and a series of four films on the theme of cities with the director Eric Rohmer. From the mid-1970s to the mid-1980s, he was involved in the new Pompidou Centre in Paris. During the same period, he established the Fondation Collioure in southwestern France which explores the links between cultural heritage and economic development. In 1990 he published a second book, *Parcs et jardins contemporains* (Contemporary Parks and Gardens) based on visits to designers worldwide in preparation for an exhibition on the same theme at the Pompidou Centre. The latter fell through for budgetary reasons, but Jack Lang, the Minister of Culture at the time, consulted Pigeat about setting up a new

Sculptor Serge Mansau's globe or 'Yourte' adorned the Chaumont 'Cour de la ferme' (Farmyard) in 2001. Hundreds of moulded glass leaves in a dozen different forms hung from a metal frame.

Opposite Beyond many of Chaumont's innovative creations rises the silhouette of its château. 'Woven Willows' (1995) by David and Judy Drew was one of the Festival's most influential exhibits.

government programme to promote gardens. This first involved restoring the Tuileries and Palais Royal gardens in Paris. Lang was also mayor of the city of Blois in the Loire valley where he encouraged the creation of avant-garde projects by contemporary designers. Along with the council of the Centre-Val de Loire region, he asked Pigeat to organize the first International Garden Festival of Chaumont-sur-Loire, near Blois, in 1992.

Founded at the same time as the non-profit-making association that created the Festival was a year-round institution for teaching and research, the Conservatoire international des Parcs et Jardins et du Paysage (International Conservatoire of Parks, Gardens and Landscape, known as CIPJP). Its activities are less in the public eye, but nevertheless tremendously influential all over France. The workshops for town planners offered by the Conservatoire in the winter have helped many small and rural communities improve their environments and have promoted the popular Chaumont planting style in public parks all over the country – a loose mixture of perennials, grasses and annuals comparable to current Dutch styles. The Conservatoire sponsored botanical expeditions to Chile in 1993 and to Japan in 1995 and 1996. There are shared educational projects with the University of Tours and with nearby horticultural schools in Tours and Blois. In 2002 the French Ministry of Education labelled it a *Pôle national de Ressources d'Art et Culture* (National Centre for Artistic and Cultural Resources) in the domain of gardens and landscape.

In 1992, in exchange for continuing support from the region, the Conservatoire agreed to promote neighbouring sites, to advise on their restoration, to help conduct an inventory. All this has been accomplished. Today it is busy with projects connected to having the Loire valley classified as a World Heritage Site by UNESCO. Also in 2002, Jean-Paul Pigeat was entrusted with the administration of the historic property of the Château de Chaumont. Its 19th-century park, landscaped by Achille Duchêne, now provides an experimental terrain for contemporary sculpture. The Queneau farm in the grounds welcomes groups of children all year round in an entirely new venture. An arboretum will provide opportunities for horticultural and ecological experimentation and the stables are being transformed into exhibition and performance spaces. 'It will take a few years yet for this domain to become once more the dream house it was in the early 20th century,' says Pigeat. 'But this time, it will be to benefit the public. It will offer a whole art of living.'[4]

Meanwhile, the Conservatoire's recently established design studio is creating and advising not only on the Parc de la Gloriette in the neighbouring city of Tours, but also on the French embassy gardens in Vienna, and other far-flung places. These new activities are already beginning to boost festival finances. Jean-Paul Pigeat is proud that he has never received money from the national government, though the region has helped generously, contributing 4.5 million francs (700,000 euros) in 2001. The department of Loir-et-Cher also provided a million francs (153,000 euros) in the same year, and private sponsors donate about the same in money or products. Still, nearly four-fifths of the Festival budget come from its own resources. It is this relative financial independence that, for Pigeat, guarantees freedom of expression: 'We need obey no rules, we have no obligation. If we wanted to keep on all of the gardens from one year to the next, we could do it. No one tells us what to do.'

The Place and the Plan

The Château de Chaumont is a historic property belonging to the nation, set on a steep hillside overlooking the main road that connects the cities of Blois and Tours in the Loire valley. In 1992 it was in such dire straits that some of the old trees outside the park were cut down and sold to pay bills. The three-hectare Festival site offered to Pigeat borders the historic park near a complex of 19th-century experimental farm buildings. It can be accessed from three directions:

through the farm, from the château park below or directly from the road above. More than 2,800 trees were planted the first year, notably the hornbeam hedging outlining the thirty garden plots.

The Festival's ground plan was conceived and contributed by the Belgian designer Jacques Wirtz and implemented by Michel Boulcourt. Its thirty plots of roughly 2,690 square feet (250 square metres) provide privacy for each exhibit while making it easy for visitors to compare them. Jean-Paul Pigeat likened the plan to a mosaic, a labyrinth and a formal garden all at once. Laid out like the curving branch of a tulip tree, with the garden plots as individual leaves, the design is smoothly flowing both within the plots themselves and in their sequence. It cleverly avoids taking sides in the historic opposition between the curves of picturesque parkland and the right angles of formal parterres. It also presents some challenges to participants, who must plan designs to fit a tulip- or bell-shaped space. As for visitors, the layout at Chaumont suggests an itinerary but does not impose it. Zigzagging is possible according to individual whim.

Procedures and Exhibitors

Each year's theme is announced during the summer to solicit entries in the autumn. Past themes included 'Pleasure' (1992), 'Imagination during Recession' (1993), 'Acclimatizations' (1994), 'Curiosity' (1995), 'Is Technology Poetically Correct?' (1996), 'Water, Water Everywhere!' (1997), 'Ricochet' (1998), 'Nothing but Potagers!' (1999), 'Liberty' (2000), '*Mosaïculture* and co.' (2001), 'Eroticism in the Garden' (2002) and 'Weed' (2003).

Three types of gardens are shown at the Festival today: those selected by a jury from submissions, those proposed by famous designers invited to participate, and those created by the students and trainees of the Conservatoire. The jury changes from year to year, mixing Chaumont representatives and outside guests. There is always one designer who showed the year before. In 2002 Aude Charié, Chaumont's publicist, was included. One of Pigeat's original team, Charié founded its publicity agency Papyrus – which also counts Villandry among its clients – while obtaining huge success with an invention of her own: a designer flea market.[5]

In 2002 over 450 proposals were reviewed for about 25 spaces. The jury meets in December and then a technical team evaluates projects for practicality. Construction begins in the New Year and planting takes place from 1 April. Plants for the summer Festival are grown either in the Conservatoire's own nursery or in greenhouses tended by the students of the Ecole nationale supérieure de la nature et du paysage in Blois, founded a year after and in close association with the Chaumont Festival. The students from Blois have themselves created several Festival gardens. The Conservatoire's own trainees do much of the planting, an arrangement that has advantages for everyone.

The layout of the Festival park was a gift from Belgian designer Jacques Wirtz and was implemented by Michel Boulcourt. It was inspired by a tulip tree branch with leaves.

Opposite Julia Barton's 'Erotica: les chemins de la séduction' (Erotica: The Ways of Seduction, 2002) included this provocative rosette of steel points emerging from a carpet of alternanthera. The desire to touch was irresistible.

In any given year, about six of the thirty installations will be held over from the year before by popular acclaim. These have included Hiroshi Teshigahara's 'Tunnel de bambous' (Bamboo Tunnel), or Patrick Blanc's 'Murs vivants' (Living Walls, see page 136). Some have been re-created in the Chaumont 'hall of fame', the 'Jardin permanent' (Permanent Garden) established by Bernard Wolgensinger. Each exhibitor is endowed with the same sum, unchanged since the early years: 80,000 francs (12,196 euros) per garden or 100,000 francs (15,245 euros) including designer fees. Some participants, like Simone Kroll who worked with school children on the early kitchen gardens, are proud of staying well below this figure. In rare cases, outside help from sponsors may be allowed: faced with high transport costs to bring century-old tree trunks from western France for the 'Trognes' (Pollards) exhibit, Dominique Mansion held a public meeting in Vendôme to find sponsors offering a further 50,000 francs (7,622 euros). Some were later involved in founding the Centre européen de trognes, a project that resulted from Mansion's experience at Chaumont.

Participating designers remain in charge of their own projects. Between those who have the actual construction done entirely by local contractors and the Conservatoire's gardeners, and those who do everything with their own hands, there is every possible combination. Many of the younger ones remember the camaraderie that existed among participants as the best part. Katharina Schütze of the pep Studio in Berlin writes: 'We got to meet other teams who were building their garden (and they were just as proud and excited as we were) and people who were working and living at the Conservatoire. In the evenings we cooked together in the big kitchen of the Conservatoire and had a very good time....

Eric Ossart's exuberant mixes of vegetables, herbs and flowers in the 'Cour de la ferme' (Farmyard) are now imitated all over France.

All people were working very hard every day. But still the atmosphere was full of creative forces and energy. I think none of us will ever forget this extraordinary experience.' Many, like the Belgian designer France Rossignol who exhibited in 1999 and 2000, comment on the technical and horticultural help received from the home team 'used to working in all sorts of conditions, faced with the crazy ideas which sometimes emerge from the designers.... Not only do they have a perfect knowledge of the plants and their potential, they also find imaginative solutions and create decors out of nothing. That's a bit the magic of Chaumont. You all work together for a great celebration and everyone overflows with energy to prepare for opening day.'

Many contributors pay personal homage to Jean-Paul Pigeat for his inspirational ideas and encouragement and his ability to solve problems without picky constraints. Hugues Peuvergne who built a house out of straw bales in 2000 recalls: 'Once the project passed the technical screening, I had total freedom. Someone asked, what if some smoker drops a live butt? Pigeat said they would provide extinguishers, but were not going to stop a project because it had some risks. In any case there are constant safety controls.' Peuvergne judges that 'this experience was formative and very rich. It taught me to work with a team, to take each one's knowledge into account, to be realistic about budgets and to keep in mind my main goal: offer a dream trip to the public, using the magic of plants and space.'

Others recall that total liberty and spontaneity can mean arrangements that are constantly reinvented. Letters may be answered or not. Appointments are unpredictable. Passions and polemics blow hot and cold. An American designer wanting to place plants herself arrived (after much preliminary correspondence) on a holiday weekend, found no one on site and being a resourceful person, climbed over the wall to gain access. Yet her memories are warm and her gratitude as strong. In theory all the gardens are ready by 1 June. Festival gates open a few days later and only close mid-October.

Welcoming the Public

Certain decisions were taken at the outset to ensure comfort with discretion, while allowing the public as much freedom as possible. Since the Festival site is located between the château park and a country road outside its walls, it was possible to have parking lots close by but out of view. Once inside, visitors find amenities unobtrusive. There are thirty benches scattered along the broad paths, but no dustbins. Pigeat claims that they would be ugly and counterproductive since it is their very absence which prevents the public, even children, from throwing refuse on the ground. Picnic spaces are not provided, but the restaurant aims to provide fast, good and cheap food thanks to a pasta bar (featuring home-made fare and serving all you can eat), and two very reasonable menus conceived by a talented chef, François-Xavier Bogard. Lunching at Chaumont has become yet another adventure. Pigeat wanted a restaurant that would not be banal, and would make creative use of flowers as well as vegetables and fruit, some being the produce of Festival gardens.

Even the boutique has deliberately remained understated, so much so that a visiting English public relations specialist judged that it was under-exploited. It is housed in a wooden cabin (édicule) designed for the site by trainee Hélène Buisson, who provided similar treatment for nearby restrooms. And yet, low-key as it is, the shop has had enormous success and contributes a good deal to the annual budget. In recent years a Chaumont trademark 'Jardin de la France' (Garden of France) has graced numerous objects.

The buildings surrounding the 'Cour de la ferme' ('Farmyard') have been available for use by the Conservatoire since 1996. They provide teaching and library

'La Déclaration d'amour' (The Declaration of Love, 2002) reveals an ancient Chinese statue of a reclining woman taking her ease among dahlias, daturas and water lilies.

facilities, and also act as display rooms for a subtropical greenhouse, temporary photography exhibits, professional meetings and colloquia.

Visitors to Chaumont move at their own pace, with a guide or unaccompanied, as each prefers. Young designers provide commentary for those who wish it in French, English or German. Gone are the days of uniformed functionaries who used to recite by rote in so many historic properties.

When Pigeat began, there was no middle ground between the old-fashioned management of historical monuments and the amusement park or *parc d'attractions*. Chaumont inaugurated the *parc de découvertes* (discovery park) where entertainment excites curiosity and discovery becomes a learning experience. This is one reason why children have always had a special place at Chaumont, more so perhaps than at later garden festivals. Children remain a major focus in the wave of green tourism that swept France in the late 1990s, both in the many new garden projects intended for the public and in other kinds of discovery parks. One such place is Guillaume Sonnet's highly successful Vallon du Villaret, a sculpture park in the remote Lozère in south-western France. Sonnet advertises both in camping grounds and art museums for a public ranging from seven to seventy years of age. As at Chaumont, his goal is not only to enrich the experience of individual visitors but to create a sense of community.[6]

Indeed, the new French green tourism often invites participation, even from the youngest visitors. The Belgian designer Simone Kroll created kitchen gardens in the early years, first with pupils from the local school, then with disadvantaged children from Blois. In recent years, class visits have been organized on a regular basis during the festival season but in 2002, a year-round workshop programme was inaugurated through the schools, receiving some twelve thousand pupils each year. Individual visitors with children are also enticed by projects, such as the Société Pro Urba's water jungle. Children participate here to such an extent that one British journalist urged parents to bring a change of clothes for their offspring! But she claims they all enjoyed themselves thoroughly.

Exploring the Chaumont Festival can easily take a day. There are also many temptations to return and participate in both temporary and season-long activities. Projects have included wine and perfume workshops, a 'landscape discovery trail' showing how to read vestiges of the past on the land, set up like a detective investigation, courses in innovative gardening such as decorative vegetable gardening, a trend Chaumont was among the first to promote.

Criticism

In the ten years of its existence, the Chaumont Garden Festival has gone from success to success. Its influence has certainly changed the face of gardening in France and beyond. But inevitably, the strong personal vision of a single individual invites controversy. Some, perhaps the envious, suggest that Chaumont's mix of 'the spectacular, experimental, pedagogical and mercantile' leads to 'creative and financial' ambiguities.[7] Another objection focuses on its lack of plant variety, though no one familiar with the work of Eric Ossart or Patrick Blanc could challenge

their contributions in this domain (see Chapter 2). A third criticism, most strongly voiced by militant disciples of the Ecole nationale supérieure du paysage at Versailles, condemns Chaumont's emphasis on gardens as escapist entertainment, obfuscating real problems such as the ruin of local landscapes. But others question whether Chaumont's productions are in fact gardens at all, or merely performances, installations, stage designs. France's most popular gardener, Gilles Clément, writes: 'I would call this kind of show an "outdoor art festival". A garden is first of all a gardener – a close relationship between Man and nature. It is not a décor, still less an "installation".' One could argue that these very ambiguities provide the soil in which experimentation thrives (see Chapters 3–5). Garden festivals, like landscapes and gardens generally, can be subsumed into the category that historian John Dixon Hunt calls 'exterior place-making'. And as Chaumont encourages the best contemporary talents to 'make places' with a freedom obviously cherished, one is tempted to conclude that a rose by any other name may smell as sweet…

Chaumont in particular is sometimes criticized for the discrepancy between the dream and its realization. Jean-Paul Pigeat has both his head in the clouds and his feet on the ground – a rare combination in any setting. But sometimes his own enthusiasm leads him to present the Festival in 'larger-than-life' dimensions. Of varied authorship, the texts posted on panels at the entrance to each garden maintain a style that is uniformly lyrical, fervent, whimsical, often witty, and full of cultural references and allusions. At times, however, even the best-disposed spectator has difficulty linking the garden with the written text. Where one might wish more solid information, there is a flight of fancy – a personal fancy, which is not always transferable. Pigeat's books about the Festival, having more room, do include explanatory supplements with technical details, garden plans and plant lists. Such information is also now available to some extent on the Festival website.

One of Pigeat's noblest dreams has been to reach a public from all backgrounds, regardless of social or professional hierarchies. He has certainly achieved this beyond all reasonable expectations. But can one be Givenchy and a high-street store all at once? Newspaper accounts, generally enthusiastic, assume couturier status for the Festival, making puns on *haute bouture* (cutting) or *haute culture*. This does not prevent the Parisian intellectual establishment from criticizing Chaumont's taste, raising its already high eyebrows at the garden gnomes and 'potagitis' (see Chapter 6). The general public enjoys the Festival but finds some exhibits elitist and overly conceptual, becoming impatient at times with postmodern in-jokes or technical prowess which discourages home use. Jane Amidon, author of *Radical Landscapes* (2001), judges that festival publics are ready 'to visualize garden landscapes…not as spatial entities but as malleable media of cultural commentary'. But it may be that 'malleable media' is precisely where part of the public disconnects.

With time, however, couturier ideas do filter down to the general public. 'Avant-garde' implies a delay between innovation and general acceptance (even when its inspiration may have been popular to begin with, as with Chaumont's kitchen gardens). In his books, Pigeat himself aims to provide suggestions which anyone may incorporate into a home garden of even modest ambitions, a kind of 'recipe collection' for family gardening. Many ideas have in fact gained acceptance – woven willow fencing for example – but usually after mediation through the wide-circulation gardening magazines. It is their journalists who, caught up in their own enthusiasm for the Festival, work out practical applications and help readers first pick them out, then implement them.

It is also very much to Pigeat's credit that he keeps discovering and including star talent worldwide, not only in garden design but in many related fields. There is however a communication gap here, insofar as not even the Parisian intelligentsia recognize all the famous names from abroad. As for the general public, it may come and go over a whole summer without ever grasping the international significance of figures such as Andy Cao, Adriaan Geuze or Vladimir Sitta. Might the introductory texts give a more complete background on the creators' earlier achievements? The designers themselves do not complain, though they grumble a little when titles of exhibits are invented or changed without consultation. And it is certainly true that, more than ever today, leading international figures in garden design long to be invited to Chaumont.

The Chaumont Achievement

Chaumont's warm welcome for children is not merely community involvement or a commercial choice, though both of these considerations are present. The spirit of irreverent play is also part of the Chaumont experience for adults. There have even been inventions such as Horror Days, long before the current invasion of Hallowe'en, and even one year, Nothing Days, when a visitor could be assured of a quiet visit, a bit like Lewis Carroll's unbirthdays. He would have felt quite at home at Chaumont. Alice too.

No doubt it is the Festival's roots in a coherent philosophy that make it much more than a commercial venture. Other festivals promote new ideas, techniques and young talent and offer established names a chance to create without the constraints imposed by clients. But Chaumont has also been a pioneer in opening up dialogues between 'fine art' and garden design, between conceptual landscape architecture and hands-on gardening, between elite culture and popular appeal. In its blending of didacticism and fun and in its participatory management techniques, it has provided a model for new types of tourism. The Conservatoire has been involved in preserving the garden and landscape heritage, helping rural economy, bringing city art into country settings, teaching and training generations of students.

Jane Amidon judges that the success of garden festivals 'points to a new understanding of the garden as a vehicle of contemporary investigation'. Chaumont was the first to promote this experimentation and is still the most constant, lasting longer and recurring regularly. Arnaud Maurières, whose work counts among the most original in France today, paid Jean-Paul Pigeat the ultimate tribute when he proclaimed: 'It was Chaumont that first established the right to freedom in garden design.'

The château and its picturesque park are now managed by the Conservatoire. Successful Festival exhibits are moved there for permanent display.

global ties

Garden design today is as multicultural as music. Leading landscape architects such as Peter Walker in the USA, Adriaan Geuze in the Netherlands, Peter Latz in Germany or Hungarian-born Vladimir Sitta in Australia all practise their art worldwide. All have websites in at least two languages and all have created gardens for the International Garden Festival of Chaumont-sur-Loire.

Richard Weller, Sitta's Australian partner, considers, however, that the key to contemporary landscape architecture is 'a sense of place – along with its foot soldier, site analysis…. Sense of place can lead to a global sense of the local and a local sense of the global – a mosaic of difference; a heterogeneity of local cultures local typologies.' He suggests moreover that 'new differences will, and are, emerging from globalism. New forms of difference.'[1]

One place to discover these is at the proliferating garden festivals which, as the Franco-American designer Kathryn Gustafson observes, 'expand the edges of experimentation and introduce landscape design to a greater audience'.[2] But international cross-fertilization is both desired and feared: exotic imports can be invasive, both botanically and culturally; fashions go round the world even faster than pollens and global connections may impose uniformity rather than promote diversity. Garden festivals, so far, claim the second objective.

In 1992 the Chaumont Festival was created by Jean-Paul Pigeat as an experimental laboratory on a planetary scale. In his 1990 book *Parcs et jardins contemporains* (Contemporary Parks and Gardens), Pigeat described American designers as inspired by vast landscapes, Asians by poetic narrative and Europeans too often stuck in Anglo-Italian pastiche. His admiration went to those creators who 'escape both Le Nôtre and Gertrude Jekyll', and to the Brazilian Roberto Burle Marx who for him, as for many young designers today, is a compelling model. But Pigeat's book opened with the farm of his childhood friend Piero, an artist in beard and jeans who still lives and gardens – without a telephone – in the heart of central France. Pigeat's own global vision has remained rooted in the French *terroir*. At Chaumont, the permanent Landscape Conservatoire and the seasonal Garden Festival represent, in turn, local strength and global ties: the former organization works with many small provincial communities, while the latter remains an international showcase.

Opposite above 'Trognes' (Pollards, 1999–2000) by Dominique Mansion illustrated the ancient country skill of pollarding using tree trunks salvaged from uprooted rural hedging in western France.

Opposite below Nico Bouts and Pascale Gaucher of the Nord-Sud Paysages agency in northern France took inspiration from the hop fields of their region to create 'Houblon: dans tous les sens' (Hop: In Every Way, 1996).

Right Experiments with techniques both ancient and avant-garde have included 'La Serre molle' (The Soft Greenhouse, 1998) of Duncan Lewis and Edouard François.

world tour

Though the Chaumont Festival is international in both its inspiration and its influence, participants may use it to affirm local identity. This is the mosaic model – a union of various fragments, each retaining its distinctive character. Exhibitors must transport and concentrate their 'spirit of place' like a bouillon cube, and transform the century-old heritage of an entire culture into a one-season installation.

Several ways of doing this have emerged since it started. Some designers simply create a garden of comparable or reduced size, as it might be found at

home. Typical of a local style, it has the added 'zip' of a contemporary creator's vision. Thus, garden styles from China, the USA, Portugal and Algeria have all been represented at Chaumont.

Another approach links local character to regional products which are easily identified by the passing public. In their classification of narrative landscapes, Matthew Potteiger and Jamie Purinton describe this as 'the souvenir, where a piece or a part acts, much like a synecdoche, as a reminder or representation

In the 'Jardin congolais' (Congolese Garden, 1999) Belgian designer France Rossignol used dyed wood chips, pine bark, pottery shards and charcoal to recreate the beautiful patterns of African art.

Left Cultural identity in capsule form draws on popular associations. The 1999 'Potager portugais' (Portuguese Garden) was designed around striking columns of Azulejos pottery.

of a larger event or place.' Thus 'Bipergorria' (Red Pepper, 2000) evokes the powdered spice made from hot Espelette peppers near Bayonne in a garden that uses the Basque colours of red, white and green. This display was sponsored in part by the Espelette pepper producers' union. Hop vines in 'Houblon: dans tous les sens' (Hop: In Every Way, 1996) evoking Flemish beer, created a futuristic jungle in an exhibit designed by the Nord-Sud Paysages agency.

Cultural tourism, part of the world's number-one industry, imposes the same constraints on garden

to visitors, or when advertising links a product to a place. But he notes nonetheless a 'new and extremely widespread sensitivity' to the connection between landscape and sense of self. Garden festivals allow designers to raise these issues in a context that is not immediately commercial, but nevertheless reaches a wide public.

Festival gardens that aim to assert regional character can be compared with the controversial traffic roundabouts visible today outside the smallest French village. Both display in a limited, predetermined space whatever constitutes the community's main source of pride, and both are contested by the cultural establishment. However, as miniature garden-and-landscape statements of local values, they have interesting similarities.

Such concentrations of regional imagery for outside consumption are of course familiar from the World's Fairs of the past. How rich in associations then was the 'Jardin congolais' (Congolese Garden) designed at Chaumont in 1999 by France Rossignol. She took inspiration from a garden imagined for the 1958 World's Fair by the doyen of Belgian landscape architecture, René Péchère. At the time, Péchère found no easy African garden model so imitated fabric patterns instead. Carefully avoiding colonialist condescension, Rossignol elegantly re-created 'the beauty and diversity of these popular African arts'[3] with the help of dyed wood chips, pine bark, pottery shards and charcoal.

In the 'Potager impérial chinois' (Imperial Chinese Garden, 1999) the font resembled a Western focal point but in fact space was organized according Taoist symbolism.

festivals as elsewhere: artists must catch the sympathies of a fast-moving, cosmopolitan public travelling with uncertain knowledge and vague assumptions. Is integrity thereby endangered? Does catering to tourists, even the culturally motivated, cheapen, spoil or dilute any 'authentic' dialogue? The historian Alain Corbin describes how landscape preservation, now 'a strong expression of local and collective identity', may lead to a certain 'theatricality of attitudes' when locals feel that they are performing

tartan potager

tarpot 1999 Lumir Soukup, Nigel Buchan and Frazer McNaughton, Scotland

In 1999, the kitchen garden theme produced a good crop of national flavours. Much acclaimed was the witty 'Tartan Potager' or 'TarPot', which played with images of Scottish identity. Nigel Buchan heads the landscape architecture section of the Scottish Natural Heritage where Frazer McNaughton is also engaged. Lumir Soukup, whose father emigrated from Czechoslovakia in 1948, trained at the Glasgow School of Art before studying landscape architecture at the University of Edinburgh. His most famous work before Chaumont was the Bathgate Face on the site of a former British Rover car factory. For this, 1,216 local faces were measured and the results combined into a collective design 98 feet (30 metres) across, an earthwork constructed out of waste concrete, builders' rubble, earth, grass and wildflowers. Local character communicated through art is one of Soukup's specialities. But 'TarPot' at Chaumont was McNaughton's idea.

The acronym 'TarPot' was a way of mocking facile labelling, an ironic inversion of the souvenir approach. The 'Chaumont clan' colours were laid out in bands of 1,650 bright hybrid vegetables set in contrasting mulch: various cabbages (dwarf, curly-leafed cabbage 'F1 Charmant', red cabbage 'F1 Perfection') blended with the vivid tones of red-ribbed chard and annual sage (*Salvia splendens* 'Carabinière Rouge'). A zigzag strip of Scottish 'wildwood' penetrated the pattern like lightening, mingling hazel, Scots pine, birch, elder and rowan, all rising from a carpet of ferns. A raised metal platform afforded an overall view through an arch of wire baskets, which contained objects representing Scotland. This was a bothy, which Soukup defines as 'traditional Scottish shelter usually found in remote, wild landscapes for

Opposite 'TarPot' was a commentary, both ardent and ironic, on Scottish nationalism. It was created by two landscape architects and an artist.

Above 'The bothy,' explains Lumir Soukup, contained 'little fetish objects, small assemblages of different materials or objects that carried a conceptual message of some kind.'

Right Red-ribbed chard, kales and cabbages, shallots and onions mixed with bright red sage and feathery ferns to provide the main colour scheme.

The 'TarPot' plan shows the strip of 'wildwood' composed largely of birch, pine, hazel, elder and mountain ash. Heather would not grow in Chaumont's alkaline soil.

Above right Strips of purple, green and red vegetables, most of them commonplace in Scottish cuisine, composed the tartan patterning visible from the platform of the bothy.

passing travellers (shepherds, drovers, etc.). For the garden in Chaumont there was something very attractive about the idea of building a "shelter" out of ideas and images. To use a traditional form, updated, to explode a whole series of clichés.' Objects were contributed by eminent Scots, such as the novelist Alasdair Gray, the film-maker Felicity Johnstone, the choreographer David Smith, the architect and sculptor Matthew Inglis and the garden designer Claudia Ferguson-Smyth. Thus the 'Flower of Scotland' was represented by the opium poppy, beer cans of a favourite brand stood for 'Brave Heart' and vinyl disks of bagpipe music hung next to Elvis Presley music. National identity trembled between archaic cliché and multinational exchanges, not

Above This garden with a message made an impact because of its aesthetic appeal, depending very much on careful attention to detail, particularly textures.

Left The designers constantly exploited contrasts between natural and man-made elements, tradition and technology. In only 250 square metres they represented wilderness, agriculture and the kitchen garden.

Below Like many artists working at Chaumont, the three Scots found creative solutions for incorporating the existing trees, slopes, water – or lack of it – into their plot.

always positive. The designers' advice was to 'Compost…compare…comment.'

'TarPot' was later re-created in the University of Edinburgh's Round Room gallery – official recognition indeed! The following year Lumir Soukup helped to establish Scotland's first Temporary Garden Festival and is now hard at work on the gardens of the new Scottish parliament – under the direction of the Barcelona agency of Enrico Morales. Part of Scotland's hard-won individuality is a sense of irony.

new england garden

1994 Lynden B. Miller, USA

Lynden B. Miller created for Chaumont 'a New England country garden very much like my own in northwest Connecticut' with 'a white wooden picket fence, rose arbor, country chairs and a bench which I adapted for American gardens from an old love-knot bench at Hatfield House in England.' She interpreted the year's theme of 'Acclimatization' historically, choosing 'American plants which, during the last few decades, have been improved upon by European growers, given cultivar or varietal names and returned to American gardeners with a new cachet from their trip to the Old World. One could say that they have had the European tour, so *de rigueur* for American intellectuals and artists. The plants returned more cultivated and were re-acclimatized with new titles and pedigrees. New England Asters, Eupatoriums, Rudbeckias and Solidagos are some plants in this category.' The wooden armchairs also resulted from transatlantic exchanges: first designed in 1918 by the Dutch craftsman Gerrit Rietveld, they were later adapted in the 1960s by the American Lester Collins.

Miller was for many years a painter who, before coming to garden design, created 'abstract collages of landscape'. She viewed her work at Chaumont as 'a giant collage of colours, shapes, textures and forms' stressing summer and autumn flowering varieties. She wanted above all a garden meant for enjoyment and came herself several times to choose and place the plants. The result was not American colonial, but perhaps reminiscent of the 1920s revival. This mode was characterized (according to historian Mac Griswold) by formal layouts almost obscured by a luxuriance of flowers, 'punctuated with urns, sometimes bristling with yucca…' as in Miller's garden at Chaumont. The women who created these gardens were designers, writers and founders of the first Garden Club of America, worthy ancestors of a designer who today combines strong regional roots with global awareness.

Miller's incorporation of tradition into contemporary design is evident in the public park plantings with which she has blessed the city of New York (the Conservatory Garden of Central Park, Bryant Park, parts of Battery Park City and many more). After the World Trade Center disaster of

11 September, noting the spontaneous use made by New Yorkers of their green spaces as memorials, she promoted the planting of one million yellow tulips and daffodils to create commemorative ribbons of yellow throughout the city for spring 2002. She believes deeply in the regenerative value of gardens.

Miller's design had two goals: 'transposing painting into the garden and illustrating the acclimatization of American plants in Europe, many later reintroduced into America.'

Red foliage (perilla, cotinus) set off summer and autumn flowers like *Verbena bonariensis*, *Sedum spectabile*, coreopsis, golden rod and rudbeckia, along with cottagey annuals (petunias, nicotiana and zinnias).

Left Miller is aware that globalization did not begin in our time. The 'New England Garden' is not nostalgic but a reminder of how plants and styles have been travelling for centuries.

skills and inventions

Art historians suggest that forms travel, changing meanings as they go. The same might be said of techniques. During his pre-festival scouting, Jean-Paul Pigeat noted in the greenhouses of the United Arab Emirates a special misting device which, he found, was manufactured in northern France by the Dutrie company. With the latter's help, he developed an ornamental variant using colder water for denser effects. Artificial fog transformed for aesthetic reasons first appeared in France at the Parc de La Villette in Paris, then in 1992 at the first Chaumont Festival.

The Festival has always concentrated on skills and inventions, whether to preserve ancient ways, recycle industrial inventions for artistic purposes or explore new directions. The education courses offered by the Chaumont Conservatoire include one entitled Old and New Technologies. Chaumont's conservationist dimension is often overlooked, but the Festival has illustrated endangered crafts to help keep them alive. Many of these techniques reappear from country to country. Thus, the Atelier Kaba (Team Zoo) experimented with raw earth construction as practised both in Japan and in the Sologne province of France ('Jardin de Terre', Earth Garden, 1994-95). In 'Sillon romand' (Swiss Furrow, 1996), designers from the city of Lausanne illustrated the farmer's planting technique of *planon*, where poplar or willow branches are directly inserted into a hedgerow. Tree pruning for firewood, an age-old and near universal custom, was studied by Dominique Mansion in 'Trognes' (Pollards, 1999–2000) using tree trunks, 'natural gargoyles' over two hundred years old. Woven wicker fencing dates at least from early Roman times, and today commonly serves to hold in riverbanks and roadside plantings. At Chaumont, students of the Ecole méditerranéenne des jardins et du paysage de Grasse with designer Arnaud Maurières used them to make a beautifully patterned rice paddy for 'La Rizière' (The Rice Paddy, 1997). *Froissartage*, a modern technique for assembling wooden pieces into anything from furniture to bridges was named after Michel Froissart who invented it in the 1930s. Every boy scout learns this technique, but architect Harold Schmitt introduced it to Chaumont to create a suspended passageway over a jungle of tree ferns in 'Passerelle dans la jungle' (Jungle Footbridge, 1996). As for the intricate bedding skills of *mosaïculture*, they inspired the theme for a whole year of gardens in 2001.

Recycled industrial techniques appeared in many exhibits in 1996 to illustrate the theme 'Is Technology Poetically Correct?' Eric Ossart used gabions – stones piled inside wire netting – to imitate ancient Mediterranean ruins, a mock Saracen tower or Roman fragments. The rounded shape was particularly difficult to obtain, and its construction provided the basis for a teaching workshop for the Conservatoire.

Contemporary technology has produced a rich crop at Chaumont too of course, from fibre optics to the Kevlar mesh canopy used by Swiss explorer Gilles Ebersolt for his famous 'Radeau des cimes'

The Atelier Kaba (Team Zoo) is a group of Japanese architects who work against hierarchy, formalism and ideologies, but promote marriages of ancient lore and modern technology. Here the 'Jardin de Terre' (Earth Garden, 1994–95).

(Treetop Raft), adapted here by Patrick Blanc as a pergola for a collection of climbing convolvulus (1996). A Persian invention for collecting dew, still used in the Canary Islands, became a beautiful patterning of gauze cones in 'Mignonne, allons voir si la rosée' (Darling, Let Us See If The Dew, 1998). Architect Edouard François, famous for his 'flower towers' intermingling buildings and live plantings – as at the Château Le Lez apartment complex in Montpellier – has often experimented at Chaumont. In 1998 he and his British colleague Duncan Lewis produced 'La Serre molle' (The Soft Greenhouse) where plastic was draped over bamboo poles leaning crazily in all directions, like something in a Dali painting.

Often at Chaumont techniques are specifically offered as models of ecology and economy. Helen Keller International's 'Gardens for Bangladesh' showed the public a self-sustaining home garden from the monsoon-drenched alluvial plains of the Bay of Bengal. 'Home Gardening' is an HKI sponsored programme to help poor rural populations cultivate crops rich in vitamin A, such as squashes, leafy vegetables, carrots and sweet potatoes, to combat deficiencies which cause the death of two million children a year and the irreversible blindness of 350,000 more. In 1995 another exhibit was straightforwardly entitled What is a Garden For? and demonstrated water purification through a series of ponds with filtering plants ('A Quoi sert ce jardin, ce jardin sert aqua?' or 'Lagugnages'). This technique is regularly used at the Terre Vivante centre in the French Alps, a foundation with gardens designed by Gilles Clément. A tireless explorer of planetary perspectives, Clément has long defended his own vision of the local-global dialogue: 'Every piece of earth is a piece of The Earth, every garden is a fragment of a much larger garden, the entire planet.'[4]

Above The 'Gardens for Bangladesh' by Helen Keller International (1999) shows how the family plots of Bengalese farmers can incorporate traditional methods of cultivation and construction and become self-sustaining.

Left 'Gabions' by Eric Ossart (1996) used a common building technique to create a poetic mood. A great variety of largely silver foliage plants complemented the play of light on mock romantic ruins.

square foot gardening

l'art du potager en carrés 1999 Jean-Paul Collaert and
Jean-Michel Wilmotte, France

In the 1960s in Santa Cruz, California, a gardener
named Alan Chadwick began experimenting with
intensive organic methods to increase yields both
for home gardens and small farms. By the mid-
1970s, west-coast gardeners were widely copying
his techniques in small-scale 'raised-bed plantings'.
Invariably cited as precursors were Swiss philosopher
Rudolf Steiner's biodynamic approach and professional
gardens outside Paris in the 1890s. These were
the same French market gardens already admired
in 1869 by English horticulturalist William Robinson
for their 'very fresh' produce, grown on 'the best and
most thoroughly cultivated patches of ground I have
ever seen. Every space of the earth is at work.' They
produced up to eight crops a year on a single tiny plot.

   One of the many west-coast books on this
theme was called *Square Foot Gardening* by
Mel Bartholomew.[5] In France it inspired Jean-Paul
Collaert, once a market gardener himself in the
Dordogne. Today one of France's leading garden
writers, Collaert developed with his friend Eric Pradine
a contemporary version of the gardening and a book
describing it, both called *L'Art du Potager en Carré*.
Still present in their adaptation are the small raised
beds of rich soil which heat up fast in spring and
allow rapid replacement of crops as harvested.

   The garden created by Collaert at Chaumont
was strikingly chic, thanks to glowing metal containers
designed by renowned French architect Jean-Michel
Wilmotte. Known to Parisians for *Le Mur pour la paix*
(Wall for Peace) on the Champs de Mars, Wilmotte
has also updated parts of the Louvre and the Palais
de l'Elysée. Always noted for minimalist mastery of
space and light, he imagined for Chaumont garden
units that would allow some squares to be shaded,

In the 1970s, Californians took inspiration from the intensive
methods of French 19th-century market gardeners. Today Jean-Paul
Collaert and Eric Pradine have brought the method back to France.

Opposite Leading architect Jean-Michel Wilmotte created
imaginative structures for this potager which illustrated his command
of graceful design and his mastery of light sculpting form.

Far right Square foot gardening in raised beds offers many practical
advantages including easy cultivation for the elderly, and a chance
to provide each crop with what it most needs.

some to be covered in glass, some to have lattices and frames, and all to be watered according to individual needs with soaker hoses. These containers constituted ideally sized beds – 13 square feet or 1.2 square metres – further subdivided into nine squares, each filled with a different crop. Collaert has long promoted the intermingling of flowers, herbs and vegetables, both for companion planting and for purely decorative reasons. Pleasing patchworks were created here using purple basil, frilly batavia and massive romaine lettuces, borage for its bright blue flowers, multi-coloured cabbages and peppers, fennel and strawberries, eggplant and chives, 'Golden Teepee' beans, and an F1 tomato hybrid named – in keeping with the futuristic design – 'Supersonic'!

walls of palestine

murs de palestine 2000–2002 Bruno Marmiroli, Walid azme al-Houmouze, Patrick Genty, Veronica Alcacer, France and Palestine

Terraced landscapes can be found from China, through the Mediterranean, to South America. Farmers clearing their land made walls with stones extracted from the soil, thus shoring up earth for cultivation. Andy Goldsworthy, who learned this skill from the farmers of Cumbria, turned dry-stone constructions into a fine art. A team from Chaumont first tried its hand in Palestine in 1999 as part of the French government's Mission 2000 project. With the help of local workmen they created five 'Terraces of the Nativity' in the Artas valley, which required 54,000 square feet (5,000 square metres) of stone. Jean-Paul Pigeat selected for the project Bruno Marmiroli, who was then working for a Palestinian ministry restoring ancient sites near Bethlehem, while at the same time writing a thesis in anthropology. Chaumont's technical director Patrick Genty organized the planting of citrus, fig and olive trees. Palestinian mason Walid azme al-Houmouze and his men saw to the building work. Neighbours donated ancient olive trees and truckloads of manure, plus ample help and advice. Yasser Arafat inaugurated the site in November 1999 and hopes were high, but subsequent events have prevented further developments: the foundation of a landscape school in Jericho and a second project at Nazareth.

In 2000, although still based in the Middle East at the time, Marmiroli created the Palestinian garden

Above Chaumont's first venture into building dry-stone walls took place in Palestine. The chosen site of the Artas valley is near the pools of Solomon, giant cisterns dug out some 2000 years ago.

Left This terraced garden was intended as part of a Millennium peace celebration, along with creations planned by gardeners of the Conservatoire in Bethlehem, Palestine, and Nazareth, Israel.

Mediterranean plants were carefully selected for a wild look and further enhanced by spiky metal sculptures by Veronica Alcacer.

Left The Franco-Palestinian team working at home at Chaumont tried to create the effect of terracing on flat ground, using the ancient building techniques.

at Chaumont. Walid azme al-Houmouze came from Palestine to participate and in March, everyone began three weeks of intensive labour. The result was a condensed landscape of great beauty. It also became a sculpture on the theme of light when its massive mineral presence was leavened by filters of Hebron glass – the work of artist Veronica Alcacer. Patrick Genty – now Miramoli's partner in a design firm – stressed grey-leafed plants with blue and white flowers to echo the tones typical of Mediterranean landscapes: the annual blue-flowered sage *Salvia patens* as well as its less common variant *S. patens* 'White Trophy', the wildly rampant *Salvia uliginosa* intermingled with fragrant nicotiana, arborescent heliotrope and anthemis 'Filament d'argent'. Bulbs and grasses were represented by *Gladiolis callianthus* 'Murieliae' and *Pennisetum villosum*. It was possible to climb along the top of the wall to explore, much as one might examine a ruin in an unfamiliar field; but the path in fact led nowhere, being not a passage but an end in its own right, forcing inspection and admiration of the edifice. 'Murs de Palestine' was maintained for the 2002 Festival as a plea for peace in an ever more troubled part of the world.

Empty and full spaces, curves and corners here serve design purposes, whereas in a Mediterranean landscape they espouse the topography, making each terrace different from its neighbour.

The Palestinian garden at Chaumont strikes a note of exciting exoticism, like a fragment of foreign soil set down in the Loire valley.

Left Bruno Marmiroli feels that most architects lack contact with their materials. Dry-stone construction requires intimate exploration of each stone.

fusion gardens

Many gardens cited in this chapter could be called 'fusion gardens' in their blending of worldwide sources and references. The term expresses the melting-pot model rather than a mosaic of discrete parts. There are other expressive metaphors for intermingling. Weaving inspired three young women from the Ecole nationale supérieure de création industrielle (ENSCI). The industrial design course taken by Eve Girardot, Laeticia Anglade and Sophie Breuil does not normally include gardens but does place emphasis on fabrics. The title of their garden 'Mé-tissage', realized at Chaumont in 1999, was deliberately punned on *métissage*, a term meaning 'crossbreeding' in animal husbandry and evoking racial mixes in human beings. At the same time it contains the word for weaving, *tissage*. Crops were planted in bands and strips on a variety of geo-textiles, which represented the various soils of the earth. Richard Weller also views 'landscape as fabric and fabrication in which natural and synthetic threads form new materials and new identities – hybrid products.'

A 1994 exhibit at Chaumont reminds us that globalization has been going on for centuries. The celebrated Blumeninsel Mainau collection in Germany presented 'Mappemonde' (Garden of the World). Plants from five continents surrounded a huge globe planted with summer blooming flowers like *Begonia semperflorens* 'Ascot Sharlach' for the Americas, *Lobelia erinus* 'Cambridge Blue' for Europe, *Iresine herbstii* for Africa and so on. This display illustrated gardens created by Count Lennart Bernadotte around his great-grandfather's collection of plants begun in 1853.

Travel and gardening – changing places and tending one piece of land – are apparent opposites which constantly meet. Garden festivals offer many new ways of moving round the world while staying in one place.

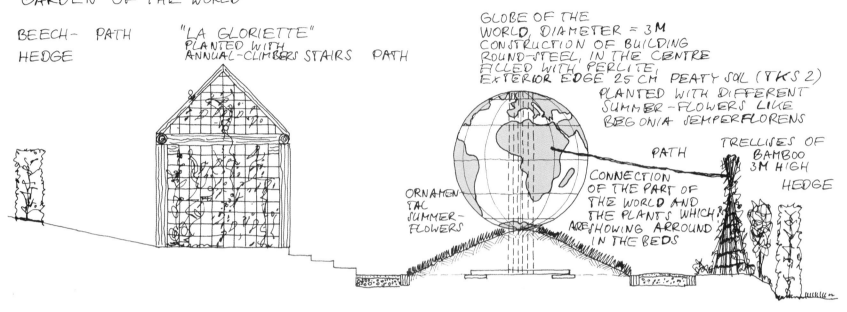

FESTIVAL INTERNATIONAL DES JARDINS EN CHAUMONT SUR LOIRE

ILE OF MAINAU

"GARDEN OF THE WORLD"

BEECH- PATH   "LA GLORIETTE"
HEDGE   PLANTED WITH
                      ANNUAL-CLIMBERS STAIRS   PATH

GLOBE OF THE
WORLD, DIAMETER = 3M
CONSTRUCTION OF BUILDING
ROUND-STEEL, IN THE CENTRE
FILLED WITH PERLITE,
EXTERIOR EDGE 25 CM PEATY SOIL (TKS 2)
PLANTED WITH DIFFERENT
SUMMER-FLOWERS LIKE
BEGONIA SEMPERFLORENS

PATH   TRELLISES OF
              BAMBOO
              3M HIGH
              HEDGE

ORNAMENTAL
SUMMER-
FLOWERS

CONNECTION
OF THE PART OF
THE WORLD AND
THE PLANTS WHICH
ARE SHOWING ARROUND
IN THE BEDS

The Blumeninsel botanical gardens of Mainau erected a giant globe some 10 feet (3 metres) in diameter on the site where Fernando Caruncho's gloriette still stood.

Left Different parts of the garden and globe corresponded to different parts of the world: Mediterranean Europe, Asia, Australia and New Zealand, the Americas and Africa.

Opposite In 'Mé-tissage' (1999) planted strips were linked together to suggest communication through weaving. The undulating movement of growing plants was accentuated by a carefully placed bent rattan substructure.

gaspacho

gaspatio andaluz 1999 Emmanuel Jalbert, Annie Tardivon,
Mahaut Michez, Laurence Delorenzi, Frédéric Reynaud from
the In Situ agency, France

With 'Gaspatio Andaluz', French designers paid
tribute to Spain by evoking one internationally
known image of that country: its famous soup.
Their proposal took the form of a recipe 'for 150,000
visitors'. The list of ingredients called for 13,000 litres
of water and a highly international blend of vegetables
ranging from Chinese cucumbers to Bernese,
Genoese, American and black Crimean tomatoes.
All of this was grown in twenty-five gleaming olive-oil
drums set in a shallow reflecting pool surfaced with
black asphalt, 426 feet (130 metres) across and
6 inches (15 centimetres) deep. The drums 62½
inches high and 27 inches in diameter (160 and 70
centimetres) were filled with broken terracotta topped
with good garden soil. Stainless-steel spirals, which
looked like unravelling containers, wound upwards
to connect with discreet overhead cables, thus
providing unusual supports for the growing plants.
Thai basil and French garlic filled two angles of the
plot beyond the pool. The whole composition was
spectacularly colourful and evolved well throughout
the season.

There were also complex games with space
and perspective as one might expect from Emmanuel
Jalbert and Annie Tardivon, founders of the In Situ
agency, graduates of the Ecole nationale supérieure
du paysage at Versailles and former interns of
Alexandre Chemetoff and Michel Courajoud. Thus,
visitors penetrated into the heart of the water garden
on two 'diving boards' reaching from either side, but
not quite touching, and springy under the feet. One
corner of the garden simply overflowed its boundary
line, extending beyond the hornbeam hedge onto
the path. A shiny white cement wall transected the

garden to create a patio effect, catching moving
shadows and reverberating heat towards the plants.
Its north side was painted blue and faced a shaded
path surfaced with a thick and fragrant layer of olive
pits from a tapenade factory in Nîmes. From this
hidden space, visitors could peep through holes
and spy on each other across the garden.

But above all, the garden remained sensuous.
Strong contrasts of sun and shade, heady scents
and interesting textures – these typically

Mediterranean pleasures encouraged visitors to
move on to the nearby restaurant to taste the soup
itself. The garden's very materials (olive-oil drums
and pits) reinforced the Mediterranean food theme
while observing the Chaumont custom of using
cheap, reclaimed materials. The welcome blurb
ended with an invitation to dream of a trip to
Spain next summer. The garden's focus was thus
unashamedly touristic, even as it poked gentle
fun at its own facile associations.

Above and left Recycled stainless-steel storage drums seem to dissolve in the reflecting pool below and unwind into a spiral above, providing support for the tomatoes. Tomato varieties included a colourful mix of modern hybrids and heirloom treasures, including 'Banana Legs,' 'Costofuto Genovese', 'F1 Grinta', 'F1 Pepe', 'F1 Pink Debut', 'Tigerella' and 'Yellow River'.

Opposite The In Situ agency created a garden full of surprising viewpoints, combining humour with technical prowess. They won the French Landscape Trophy award in 1997.

'Desert Sea' suited the 2001 *mosaïculture* (carpet bedding) theme, thanks to its multi-cultural inspiration and strongly delineated patterns. Its sensuous labyrinthine qualities also illustrated the 2002 theme of eroticism.

Right At first, visitors were invited to enter the garden and even to meditate there, but many removed the glass marbles and thereafter only an external, theatrical point of view could be allowed.

Opposite Andy Cao has become the champion of recycled glass as an alternative landscape medium. He won the Prince Charitable Trusts Rome Prize Fellowship in Landscape Architecture for 2001–2002.

desert sea

Andy Cao and Stephen Jerrom 2001–2002, USA

Andrew Thanh-Son Cao makes gardens out of glass – recycled, polished and brilliantly coloured. With the help of his partner Stephen Jerrom, he creates landscapes which are old, new and timeless all at once. He explains how memories affected their own

garden at Echo Park in Los Angeles: 'When I was ten years old my family moved from busy, urban Saigon to my grandmother's farm. Suddenly I was surrounded by ancient icons: vast rice fields set in a patchwork grid of mud banks; the rituals of harvest

as we piled rice along Highway One to dry in the humid sun. There were contemporary icons too: giant metal skeletons in the form of rusting armaments left over from the war which still dot the Vietnamese countryside today. And I remember the strange reflecting landscape of salt farms – their surreal expanse of white cones changing with the light. I have included all these images in my garden.'

For Chaumont in 2001, the partners shipped 7 miles (11 kilometres) of Manila rope and 10 tons of glass to France, both in the form of cobalt glass pebbles and hand-blown glass bubbles. Their plot still contained the bamboo groves remaining from Hiroshi Teshighara's tunnel (see p. 109). Around three sides, Cao placed 6-foot-high (2-metre) rope fences to 'serve as a backdrop and bring all the elements together'. A miniature landscape was laid out in this intimate, theatrical space with swathes of brilliant blue sea surrounding a white, rope-wrapped desert island planted with prickly cacti. Beyond, glass bubbles on rope-wrapped pedestals, irregularly spaced, were studded with small cacti and echeveria. Their graceful elongation evoked for Cao both the necks of African tribal women and Vietnamese water puppets. The overall layout echoed the dry garden of Ryoan-ji in Kyoto, with its stretches of sand replaced by 'water' made of glass.

Cao imagined visitors moving through the brilliant exoticism of this mini-labyrinth to enjoy 'the experience of walking on glass, to hear the crunch, feel the texture, and completely immerse themselves in this theatre environment'. A 20-foot (6-metre) bench offered opportunities for enjoying 'the intense but calming effect of the cobalt blue'. Cao is drawn to meditation, citing as a precedent the use of stained glass in 'religious iconography and contemplative spaces'. He imagines glass as an artistic medium in 'healing gardens and environmental art' and also wants to explore its practical garden uses, as mulch for example. However, Jerrom points out that Andy's work is 'lots of fun, and sexy too, if you look below the surface…'.

what plants
can do

Western gardening in the 20th century was dominated by English horticulture – the painstaking orchestration of choice plants into graded tableaux. Borders, floral and mixed, were composed like paintings. Today's horticulturalists still emphasize plant associations though many prefer a wilder look, which in Britain is called naturalistic. Painting still supplies a powerful model however: witness the raised viewing platform in Dutch artist Tor der Linden's garden which provides an ideal distance and angle of vision for enjoying a particular floral composition. Such an approach to garden design implies or even imposes a distance between the spectator and the scene observed. It remains predominantly visual.

Indeed, much of modern horticulture perpetuates the carefully planned perspectives of an earlier picturesque tradition on a more intimate scale. But larger scenes continue to appeal. Plants may be associated to cover whole landscapes, creating large islands of artificial wilderness (woodland) or idealized countryside (meadows). In Germany, such plantings were first conceived with conservationist motives, modelled after scientifically determined biotopes or assemblages found growing in nature. It has been said that the Germans prize ecology and the British aesthetics, while the Dutch strike the perfect balance between the two. The Dutch approach has spread, and most people now want beautiful gardens, large or small, with a clear conscience.

The French first achieved renown as botanists rather than horticulturalists, though there are many beautifully planted French collections – from as early as the period following the Second World War – which deserve to be better known. The current generation of place-makers in France are confirmed horticulturalists, drawing on a recent surge of specialist nurseries. Two plantsmen who shared in the Chaumont adventure from its early years count among France's leading examples today: Patrick Blanc and Eric Ossart – France's answer to Piet Oudolf!

A garden festival like Chaumont necessarily stresses design and technique and risks being accused of neglecting plants, though plant lists in Latin, French and English are posted at the entrance to each garden. Anyone studying Chaumont's history must, however, acknowledge the impressive variety exhibited at the Festival over the years. In 1994 and 1999, when the Festival's themes were 'Acclimatizations' and 'Nothing But Potagers!' respectively, press releases boasted of 1,500 different species and varieties on show for each season. Chaumont has even helped to organize plant-hunting expeditions to Chile and Japan, led by Patrick Blanc. Collections assembled at Chaumont have later been shown at the Courson plant fair and established at the Muséum nationale d'Histoire Naturelle in Paris. Meanwhile, the free-wheeling Chaumont planting style mixing grasses and annuals with perennials, largely created by Eric Ossart, has been taught in the Conservatoire classes for years and is now easily recognizable in public parks from Orléans and Limoges to Bordeaux. Ossart and Blanc have advised and participated in many festival gardens, sometimes combining efforts, as in 'Zingibérales' (Zingiberales, 1995). This offers a fresh look at the exotics often used uninspiringly in municipal plantings: hedychiums, strelitzia, hardy banana trees and cannas.

Opposite above 'Zingibérales' (Zingiberales, 1995) by Eric Ossart and Patrick Blanc helped launch the fashion for dramatic architectural foliage in France, using plants such as cannas in new ways.

Right In 'Primeval Perspective' (2000) James Fraser and Tina Febrey of the Avant Gardener agency created a surrealistic, antediluvian vision using plants native to New Zealand.

Opposite below 'India Song' was imagined by Eric Ossart with the complicity of Patrick Blanc. Both are incomparable plantsmen whose work has been enormously influential.

botany
and biodiversity

'Primeval Perspective' included hoherias (*H.angustifolia*, *H. lyallii*, *H. populnea* and *H. sexstylosa*), molinia sp. and pseudopanax (*P. chatamanicus*, *P. crassifolius*, *P. ferox*).

The plots at Chaumont have notable differences in soil, slope, existing trees and humidity. Some specialist nurseries have taken advantage of these variations to present plant collections such as the respected Maymou firm from Bayonne in 1994 and the Pépinières Desmartis for lagerstroemias in 1995. In the same year the famous aquatic plant dealer Latour-Marliac displayed its most stunning water-lilies in a pool surrounded by mixed grasses. The Yves Dupont nurseries chose a shaded humid plot with a natural pond for their collection of tree ferns from New Zealand and Tasmania (1995). To everyone's surprise, the *Dicksonia antartica* survived the winter with temperatures of -7° Centigrade and so the exhibit was maintained and enriched in 1996. Sometimes collections concentrate on a geographical origin, as in the Canary Islands gardens, or the spectacular New Zealand forest presented by the Avant Gardener agency in 2000. It was composed of hoherias and pseudopanax with, as the Chaumont blurb explained, 'long leaves, sometimes like sharks' teeth, shooting like arrows towards the sky. This plant world, at once antediluvian and visionary, haunts our imagination like a dream from our childhood.' Decking made from oak, jarra and iroko wood wove through this dense maze.

At Chaumont the tradition of plant hunting survives – though with conservationist sensitivity – in Patrick Blanc, specialist in jungle undergrowth and professor at the esteemed French national research institute, the CNRS. Most famous for the 'Murs végétaux' he first exhibited at this Festival (see p. 136), Blanc also helped create numerous botanical displays in the Chaumont spirit of fun and invention, including 'Retour de Valdivia' (Return from Valdivia, 1994) and 'Folles Ipomées' (Mad Ipomoea, 1996). The convolvulus collection presented in the latter was one of the largest in the world, assembled with the help of specialized dealers, gifts from far-flung botanical gardens and samples collected by Blanc himself in Tanzania, Uganda, Guadeloupe and Guyana. Blanc further honoured his favourite clinging vines in a song entitled *Un peu de botanique* (A Little Botany) written for his *chansonnier* friend Pascal Héni. All these lovely ladies inspired by 'intoxicating

chlorophyll' rise to the tropical sun, 'erotic heliphiles, exalted, climbing towards the sky…'. The refrain is a litany, lasting six stanzas, of enthralling Latin names.[1]

Left The Yves Dupont nursery of Orléans specialize in hardy ferns (dryopteris, osmunda and adiantum among many others). For Chaumont they experimented with giant tree ferns *Dicksonia antartica*.

Below The Yves Dupont nursery also advises on creating entire plant communities inspired by natural biotopes. Harold Schmitt designed the footbridge using the technique of *froissartage*.

amafas

le jardin d'amafas 2001 CIRAD (Centre de coopération internationale en recherche agronomique pour le développement or Centre for International Co-operation in Agronomic Research for Economic Development) with Patrick Blanc, France

'Le Jardin d'amafas' was a brightly coloured, richly textured design on the theme of international plant travel. Three raised beds, wedges of the same enveloping circle, represented America, Africa and Asia, hence the name 'Am-Af-As'. The American bed was bound in painted slats of woven wood, the African one in sheet metal and the Asian one in bamboo. Each displayed the continents' most important edible tropical plants: fruit-bearing species stood tall on the outer rim, medium-height tubers, such as manioc and yams, were planted in the middle and low-growing spices grew in front, closest to the viewer. Painted metal rods connected the beds to indicate how each species, grown in the section corresponding to its origins, had travelled elsewhere. Thus, the arches rose and dipped to show how coffee originating in Africa or tea in Asia had spread to the other two continents. This produced striking visual patterns, while providing practical support for the climbers. At the same time, it made the space more mysterious, creating a welcoming sense of penetration and enclosure.

Planting was done by botanist Patrick Blanc, veteran of eight scientific missions, which have included New Guinea, Thailand, Bolivia, Madagascar and Japan. Blanc studies plants' strategies for adapting to difficult environments. But he is also an artist, famous for his green and turquoise forelock and colour-coordinated jungle-motif shirts! His contributions to Chaumont since 1993 have also established him in the field of design.

'Le Jardin d'amafas' was not only beautiful, it was a statement about biodiversity and globalization.

Its sponsor was the CIRAD, a French scientific organization specializing in agricultural research for the tropics and subtropics of the world.[2] Its mission is to contribute towards rural development in the countries of these regions through experiment, training and dissemination of scientific and technical information, covering agricultural, veterinary, forestry and food sciences. The CIRAD's experiments with genetically modified crops have led to the destruction of some greenhouses by groups of French farmers.

The foundation insists, however, that research is the first precaution to be taken with new technologies, which aim, they claim, at sustainable agriculture. In 2001 the Festival theme was '*Mosaïculture* and co.' and the CIRAD's contribution was the symbolic and sensuous representation of global exchanges in a most positive light.

Above and left 'Le Jardin d'amafas' presented American, African and Asian food plants, grouped in three islands. The African bed was bound in sheet metal, the Asian in bamboo and the American in wooden slats. Arches linking beds showed how plants originating in one area travelled to another; the garden thus offered a forceful symbol of plant exchanges as a global mosaic.

Opposite Among many edibles from all over the world grown in this garden, tall red-leafed sugar cane was one of the most striking.

The CIRAD conducts research into tropical agronomy, some of
it controversial. Its message here was conveyed by strong design
combining sensuous pleasure and strong lines.

Plant Selection

Alpinia galanga Galangal
Ananas comosus Pineapple
Annona cherimola
  Custard apple
Annona muricata Soursop
Annona reticulata
  Bullock's heart
Artocarpus integrifolia
  Jack fruit
Carica papaya Papaya
Citronella gongonha Citronella
Curcuma longa Turmeric
Elettaria cardamomum
  Cardamom
Eugenia myrtifolia
Eugenia uniflora
  Surinam cherry
Hylocereus undatus
  Night-blooming cereus
Litchi chinensis Lychee
Manihot esculenta Tapioca
Passiflora edulis Passion fruit
Piper nigrum Black pepper
Psidium guajava
  Common guava
Taro alocasia macrorrhiza
  Giant taro
Saccharum officinarum
  Sugar cane
Solanum quitoense Naranjilla

Patrick Blanc is an internationally known expert on jungle undergrowth and published a book in 2002 resulting from his many research missions: *Etre Plante à l'ombre de la forêt tropicale* (Being a Plant in the Shadow of Tropical Forests).

garden for a hungry spirit

le potager d'un curieux 1999 Jean-Luc Danneyrolles, France

Jean-Luc Danneyrolles has been growing heirloom vegetables in Provence since 1984. To name his seed business, he borrowed the title of an 1892 book on world food history called *Le Potager d'un curieux* (Kitchen Garden for an Inquiring Mind).[3] Danneyrolles has himself published several volumes on vegetables and formed links, through Dominique Guillet's Kokopelli Association, with international seedsavers' movements. Outlawed by stringent European Union restrictions, this band of small producers combats the uniform seed production imposed by a small number of multinationals. Biodiversity is their constant theme.

In the Luberon hills of Provence, Danneyrolles cultivates eleven steep terraces without the aid of heavy machinery or chemicals and on a shoestring budget. He takes on trainees and organizes gardening workshops in local schools whenever funding allows. When he heard that the kitchen garden had been chosen as a theme at Chaumont, he dropped everything, got in his truck and drove straight to the Loire valley, where he was warmly welcomed: his project, rich both in unique savours and universal symbols, was perfect for the Festival.

In his design, four beds associated plants with the elements: leafy vegetables (water), root crops (earth), fruit (sun) and flowers (air). In the centre stood a huge gnarled olive trunk, dead since the terrible frosts of 1956, a presence symbolizing the cycle of life and death in the garden. Bright reds, yellows and blues echo the Matisse cut-outs that decorate his greenhouse in Provence, cheerful reminders of the earth's vitality, even in winter. Each of the paving materials recalled some part of Provençal heritage: pebbles from the Durance river, limestone from the Luberon and ceramic fragments from the famous Apt pottery. At home, Danneyrolles once assembled a whole mosaic of local history in this manner with the help of local schoolchildren, incorporating shards from the neolithic period to the present time, as he feels strongly that the future must be built on the past. In his workshed at Chaumont, he displayed old postcards and souvenirs along with 'outmoded' symbols using garden tools, like the Soviet hammer and sickle. 'I overdid it a bit,' he confesses, 'I just kept adding things.'

Danneryolles's creation at Chaumont was an attempt to make his ideal garden sometimes humorous, sometimes sentimental, but always generously overflowing with colours, scents and flavours. In a 'manifesto' written for the occasion Danneyrolles acclaimed a future where 'Art, Science and Religion, Spirit and Matter will overcome separations between continents and disciplines in the garden of tomorrow.'

Above Danneyrolles intermingled sensuous appeal, practicality and humour. His own Winged Victory was a watering can.

Left Mixing flowers with herbs and vegetables is typical of the 19th-century French country style still extant in many grandmothers' gardens. Gallardia is a classic.

Opposite Danneyrolles's richly coloured plant palate bore witness to his continuing commitment to biodiversity. His vocation for sharing and teaching led him to label everything carefully.

Paving materials ranged from prehistoric and Roman vestiges to contemporary pottery and bottle shards. For Danneyrolles the future must always build on the past.

The tool shed was also a miniature museum intermingling symbols of garden or agricultural origin – such as the hammer and sickle! Some described Danneyrolles's colours as Mexican or Provençal, but for him they are universal.

Plant Selection

Acanthus mollis Bear's breeches

Acanthus spinosus Armed bear's breeches

Achillea aegyptiaca Egyptian yarrow

Achillea ageratum Sweet Nancy

Achillea millefolium (Yarrow) 'Fire King'

Allium ampeloprasum Blue leek

Allium cepa 'Patate' Perennial onion

Allium chinensis Rakkyo

Allium fistulosum Welsh onion

Allium porrum var. Perennial leek

Allium ramosum Chinese garlic

Allium senescens ssp. montanum German garlic

Allium schoenoprasum Chives

Allium ursinum Wild Garlic

Aloysia triphylla Lemon verbena

Althaea officinalis Marsh mallow

Anethum graveolens Dill

Angelica archangelica Angelica

Anthriscus cerefolium Common chervil

Arctium lappa 'Takinogawa Long' Japanese burdock

Artemisia abrotanum Southernwood

Artemisia absinthium Common wormwood

Artemisia dracunculus Tarragon

Asperula odorata Sweet woodruff

Atriplex hortensis Cultivated orach

Atriplex hortensis ssp. rubra 'Cupreatorosea' Purple orach

Beta vulgaris ssp. rapacea Beetroot

Beta vulgaris ssp. cicla 'Flavescens' chard (various varieties)

Beta vulgaris ssp. maritima Maritime beet

Borago officinalis Borage

Brassica nigra Black mustard

Brassica oleracea acephala 'Daubenton' Tree cabbage

Cynara cardunculus ssp. inermis Thornless cardoon

Cynara cardunculus ssp. puvis

Chelidonium majus Greater celandine

Chenopodium bonus-henricus Good King Henry

Chrysanthemum coronarium 'Spatiosum' Chop suey greens

Cucurbita maxima 'Jack-Be-Little' Pumpkin

Cucurbita maxima 'Pomme d'or' Squash

Cucurbita pepo 'Blanche de Virginie' Zucchini

Cucurbita pepo 'Yellow' zucchini

Cyclanthera pedata Schräd. Achoccha

Filipendula ulmaria Meadowsweet

Foeniculum vulgare Common fennel

Foeniculum vulgare 'Purpurascens' Bronze fennel

Fragaria 'Gariguette' Strawberry

Fragaria 'Louis Gauthier' Strawberry

Fragaria 'Mara des Bois' Strawberry

Fragaria 'Reine des Vallées' Strawberry

Fragaria vesca semperflorens Alpine strawberry

Humulus lupulus Common hop

Hypericum perforatum St John's Wort

Hyssopus officinalis Hyssop

Ipomoea batatas Sweet potato

Lagenaria vulgaris Calabash gourd, Bottle Gourd

Lactuca sativa 'Corne du Diable' Lettuce

Lactuca sativa 'Grosse Blonde Paresseuse' Lettuce

Lactuca sativa 'Langue de Bœuf' Lettuce

Lactuca sativa 'Raphaël' Lettuce

Lactuca sativa 'Sucrine' Lettuce

Lathrys tuberosus Earth chestnut

Lavandula vera True lavender

Levisticum officinale Lovage

Lycopersicon esculentum 'Cœur de Bœuf Rouge' Tomato

Lycopersicon esculentum 'Noire de Coseboeuf' Tomato

Lycopersicon esculentum 'Blanche du Québec' Tomato

Melissa officinalis Lemon balm

Mentha Mint (10 varieties)

Myrrhis odorata Sweet Cicely

Nepeta cataria Cat mint

Origanum vulgare Wild marjoram

Oxalis tuberosa Oca, New Zealand yam

Phalaris arundinacea 'Luteo-Picta' Reed canary grass

Phaseolus coccineus Scarlet runner beam

Physalis alkekengi Bladder cherry

Pisum sativum 'Mangetout du Portugal' Pea

Plantago coronopus Buck's horn plantain

Proboscidea arenaria Sand Devil's Claw

Rudbeckia laciniata 'Double Gold'

Rumex patientia Patience dock

Rumex scutatus French Sorrel 'Large de Belleville' and purple sorrel

Ruta graveolens Common rue

Salvia lavandulifolia Lavender leafed sage

Salvia sclarea Clary sage

Sanguisorba minor Salad Burnet

Saponaria officinalis Soapwort

Scorpiurus vermiculata Common caterpillar plant

Smyrnium olustratrum Alexander

Stachys affinis Chinese artichoke

Symphytum officinale Common comfrey

Tanacetum vulgare Tansy

Tanacetum vulgare 'Crispum' Buttons

Thymus vulgare (4 varieties)

Thymus serpyllum Breckland thyme

Valeriana officinalis Common valerian

Vicia faba 'Verte de Pologne' Broad beans

Vicia faba 'Violette de Sicile' Broad beans

Vigna unguiculata ssp. unfuiculata Asparagus bean

Zea mays Ornamental maize (red and white varieties)

sensuous gardening

Since the Renaissance, ornamental gardening in northern Europe has favoured spectacle and display. Designers are now exploring alternative traditions, which have never separated ornamental and productive gardening and which thus appeal more to the other senses. In Mediterranean countries for example, the same aromatics that are clipped for ornamental use and act as windbreaks also provide scented foliage for medicinal, household and culinary purposes. Multisensual gardening has become fashionable in recent years because it also suggests immersion in the garden experience rather than mere spectatorship.

'Pleasure' was Chaumont's very first theme in 1992 and the 2002 theme was 'Eroticism in the Garden'. In the press releases for both, Jean-Paul Pigeat quoted the 19th-century French philosopher Charles Fourier's observation that 'a garden is the place where pleasure reaches its culmination'. This would suggest some degree of visitor participation.

Sensuousness in gardens is also visual and often begins with colour. Conservative landscape architects may dismiss colour for that very reason as unintellectual, superficial detailing, mere icing on the cake, dangerously vulgar. The English designer Russell Page, who loved colour nonetheless, felt he had first to determine form and structure, and could only then turn to 'colour and texture'. But for Brazilian designer Roberto Burle Marx, exuberant colour and form were indivisible right from the start. Eric Ossart also luxuriates in colour as an inseparable part of the whole creative experience: 'I love to nurture the living plant, organic matter, to revel in its texture, its shape, its structure, its colour and its fragrance.'[4]

Chaumont, always anti-establishment, has been conspicuously bright from its first year. Later festivals have included brilliant blends such as Ossart and Blanc's 'India Song' (1999), inspired by the Hindu festival *Holi* where people throw

coloured water and powders at each other. A huge yellow elephant presided. For the eroticism theme, many projects used violent contrasts of black and red, alternating with green. But there have been a large number of single-colour theme gardens: blue, white, yellow, red and even black. Sometimes one hue appears in blocks and swathes of geometric simplicity. White, the absence of colour, is no exception. American expatriate designer Mark Rudkin conceived a striking formal contrast between a field of white cosmos and a single 'White Lady Linda'

dahlia, placed off-centre; but this again necessitated distance and a fixed angle of vision. Michel and Geneviève Gallais also designed a beautiful white garden at Chaumont in 1996, contrasting grasses and free-floating blooms with massive dark topiaries.

Chaumont has in addition presented gardens where scent comes first. In 'Un Jardin de parfums' (A Perfume Garden, 1993), Eric Ossart combined heliotropes, acidanthera, 'Sambac' jasmine and annual nicotiana. His experience of the latter comes largely from the elegant plant tapestries he created for the Tobacco Institute at Bergerac in the Dordogne. But Chaumont's greatest sensuous achievement is perhaps its long series of kitchen gardens, starting with Simone Kroll's first experiments in 1992 and culminating in 1999, when potagers were the year's chosen theme for all participants. Jean-Paul Pigeat offered this as a down-to-earth answer to critics who were finding Chaumont too conceptual. He has always been a populist and what could appeal more to the general public in France than food?

Above The *Holi* spring fertility festival which inspired 'India Song' has been described as a 'period of mirthful abandon' amid a 'riot of colour.'

Left For 'India Song' Ossart included amaranthus 'Pigmy Torch', Celosia spictata 'Feather Purple', dahlias ('Wetzels Daughter'), gladioli ('Fidelio') amid bright pelargoniums and marigolds.

Opposite Susan Child balanced plant exuberance and a formal design easily adaptable to many garden situations. Cedar 'tripods' provided off-beat accents while framing the view.

scents and sense

ô de fleurs 1999 Rachid Koraïchi, Eric Ossart and Arnaud Maurières, Algeria and France

The title of this delightful garden punned on *eau*, the French word for water, and *ô*, an exclamation of admiration. It was created by celebrated Algerian sculptor Rachid Koraïchi with the help of Chaumont's garden manager Eric Ossart and his partner Arnaud Maurières. A grid of twenty-eight black-and-white ceramic basins rose on pedestals from beds of scented plants. A formal outline was imposed by the two classic criss-crossing 'rivers' of Paradise gardens – here shallow canals in terracotta paving. The sculptor's inspiration came from the Sufi poet Al-Atar who wrote 'The Language of the Birds' in the 12th century. All measurements were multiples of seven: the fountains were 19 inches wide and 27 inches high (49 and 70 centimetres). The ceramic basins were shallow like the hollows made in North African graves to catch rainwater for birds, angelic beings that connect earth and heaven, thus linking earth, water and air. Inside each basin Koraïchi had beautifully transcribed sacred texts in Arabic and Latin – backwards! This very personal calligraphy was only readable with a mirror, an effect that represented the difficulties of self-knowledge. Koraïchi deliberately tried to connect intimate enjoyment with spiritual meditation. He also sought cross-cultural connections, recalling that the image of God creating man from clay occurs in both the Christian Bible and in the Koran. The ceramics were fired by Patrick Galtier, the design added in maganese oxyde before second baking.

Ossart and Maurières considered this garden to be a *Gulistân* – a pleasure garden of colours and scents. They mixed roses with herbs chosen for their

Four shallow canals represented the rivers of Paradise, culminating in a painted tile pool. Designers Ossart and Maurières maintain a strong interest in Arabic inspiration.

Opposite Rachid Koraïchi combined here two favourite media: ceramics and calligraphy. Algerian writer Mohamed Dib wrote about his work that 'its beauty gives new life to old symbols.'

Opposite right Broken pottery shards made an unusual surfacing providing warm contrast with cool, scented plants as well as a pleasant 'crinkling' sound when walked on.

fragrance, but also for their hue and texture. Velvety purple officinal sage and prickly silver curry plant suffered from over-moist soil after planting and so were replaced with *Agastache mexicana* and the thistle Echinops 'Arctic Glow'. A row of summer-blooming African tamarix along one side protected a still, rectangular pool (no motion here, but reflection). More perfume came from higher borders of white nicotiana and trumpet-flowered daturas. 'Ô de Fleurs' was a particularly subtle and sensuous celebration of Paradise. Unfortunately it was not eternal…

Plant Selection

Acidanthera bicolor 'Murielae'

Citrus limon 'Quatre Saisons'
   Lemon

Cleome hassleriana
   'Violet Queen' Cleome

Coriandrum sativum
   'Slow Bolt' Coriander

Mentha rotundifolia
   'Variegata' Apple mint

Mirabilis jalapa 'Tea Time'
   Marvel of Peru

Ocimum basilicum
   'Purpureum' Purple basil

Pelargonium 'Attar of Roses'
   Scented geranium

Rosa 'Chartreuse de Parme'
   Rose

Rosa 'Jardin de Villandry'
   Rose

Images of desire glimpsed through windows were suggested by
Ettore Scuola's film *Una Giornata Particolare* (One Particular Day).
The structure was a kind of melting, fluid labyrinth, the plants the
objects of desire in its heart.

soft and loose

le jardin flou 2002 Pernilla Magnusson, Arola Tous Silvia Vespasiani, Sara Dauge, Luís Bisbe, Alex Aguilar, Spain

Inspired by the eroticism theme, four young members of the Beth Gali agency in Barcelona, artist Luís Bisbe and gardener Alex Aguilar imagined 'Le Jardin flou' (blurred, soft or soft-focus garden). Spectacular and subtle all at once, its layered veils created a diaphanous labyrinth with oval peepholes allowing glimpses through and beyond. Curtains were raised high to block out the sky. And yet the sky participated: whether shimmering pearl or scintillating gold, this garden lived by light.

Plants within were now illuminated, now masked, to 'provoke the senses' and create 'a game of concealment and desire'. At first, the architects wanted only one species: gypsophila, chosen for its 'light, airy aspect'. Their interest in plants remained 'architectonic and perceptual', but when they decided on an itinerary appealing to all five senses, greater variety was required. Aguilar brought catalogues to support his suggestions, and thus, says architect Pernilla Magnusson, 'a new world opened up for us'. Spectral corkscrew willows beckoned from beyond, lemon verbena wafted its penetrating scent, while other plants, like the globe thistles or the aptly named soft-shield ferns (Polystichum setiferum), offered themselves to the curious hand. Wind moving among taller specimens, such as pampas grass, created sound effects. A fine harmony evolved between setting and plants, the first an amiable, ever-changing enigma, the second, a prime temptation.

This was an all-encompassing approach to eroticism – inevitably so with such a large team. They chose suggestive design rather than portraying specific body parts and favoured, instead of the vivid

Plants with interesting structures like nicotiana were reflected many times over in ever changing light. Their scent was also captured by the diaphanous curtains.

colour contrasts used in other exhibits, an almost bridal white against a black, volcanic ground. Plants in green and white tones completed the monochrome effect. This contemporary rendering of the white garden offered mystery as well as elegance, disorientating the admirer who could no longer judge,

Every detail was debated in common by the team. It was decided to space the curtains only 31 inches (80 centimetres) apart to create a sense of enclosure.

from within or without, the garden's shape or size. The plot's very outline was engulfed and transgressed, the hedging transformed into dark, half-hidden shapes. Accentuating process rather than content, the quest led to no one point, but to an experience of voluptuous abandonment. 'Eroticism,' wrote the artists, 'is more the pursuit of desire, a promise of pleasure than its consummation.'

Plant Selection

Zone 1

Artemisia ludoviciana Western
  mugwort
Gypsophila elegans
Gypsophila paniculata 'Bristol
  Fairy' Baby's breath
Limonium latifolium
  White sea lavender
Reseda alba White mignonette
Salvia argentea Sage
Salvia coccinea 'Lactea' Sage

Zone 2

Ammi visnaga
Gaura lindheimeri 'Madonna'
Gypsophila elegans
Gypsophila paniculata 'Bristol
  Fairy' Baby's breath
Omphalodes linifolia
  Venus's navelwort
Orlaya grandiflora
Nicotiana sylvestris
  Flowering tobacco
Salvia farinacea 'Alba' Sage

Zone 3

Erigeron karvinskianus
  Vittidinia, Fleabane
Gypsophila elegans
Gypsophila paniculata
  'Bristol Fairy' Baby's breath
Heliotropium arborescens
  'White lady' White heliotrope
Ricinus communis
  'Zanzibariensis' Castor
  oil plant
Silybum marianum Milk thistle

Zone 4

Leymus secalinus Lime grass
Gypsophila elegans
Gypsophila paniculata
  'Bristol Fairy' Baby's breath
Miscanthus sinensis
  'Zebrinus' Zebra grass
Pennisetum setaceum
  African fountain grass
Stipa tenuissima Feather grass

Zone 5

Antirrhinum majus
  White snapdragon
Cerastium tomentosum
  Snow-in-Summer
Gypsophila paniculata
  'Bristol Fairy' Baby's breath
Lavatera trimestris
  'Mont Blanc' Lavatera
Salix matsudana 'Tortuosa'
  Dragon's-claw willow
Salix matsudana 'Tortuosa
  Aureopendula' Corkscrew
  willow

The Chaumont home team, especially Jean Louis Montiron, was instrumental in finding a fabric manufactured near Lyon which would have the right degree of transparency and yet reflect light.

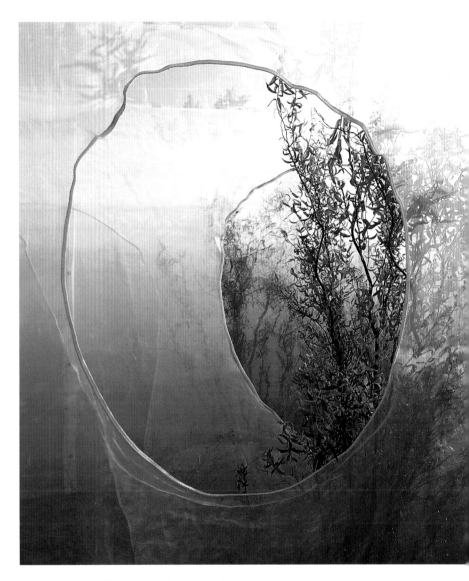

Voyeurism was a popular approach to the eroticism theme. One section here was to be tactile, one perfumed and one visual, but the distinctions soon became…soft and loose.

from texture to architecture

The intricate *mosaïculture* tradition organized bedding plants in flat or mounded spaces. The city of Blois' installation used reflecting cylinders to fuse patterns and provide vertical contrast.

One currently fashionable assemblage of plants is the wildflower meadow, a genre rich in variety, intrinsically detailed, finely textured and inherently formless. Framing is imperative, whether offered by mown paths or existing topography, as well as the contrast of vertical structures. At the other end of the scale lies the new minimalism, usually dominated by strongly defined constructions and mineral elements, with few plants – if any – and then only architectural specimens. Overlapping with the 'new classicism' or the 'modernist' garden revival, minimalists often cite formal French 17th-century gardens as precursors.

Chaumont has had many meadows. Michel Boulcourt's 'Jardin d'Eden' (Garden of Eden) of 1992 presented at first glance a simple field around an apple tree: a mix of wheat, barley and pennisetum was studded with scattered gomphrena, statice,

mixed cosmos and calendula. A second look, however, revealed a host of thin carbon-fibre rods which caught the light and moved with the grasses in the wind. The city of Lausanne exhibit of 1996, 'Sillon romand' (Swiss Furrow), presented a ploughed field with strips of lawn on one slope of each row and wild meadow plants (sage, chicory, cornflower, poppies and daisies) on the other. This contrast opposed regimented city life to country freedom. Tall upright mirrors provided vertical accents and made it possible to see both sides at once.

Minimalist gardens using only one species can still make statements about growth and variety. The tiered grey garden, 'Histoire d'agaves' (Story of Agaves), created by students from the Ecole d'architecture et de paysage in Bordeaux in 1994, showed the acclimatization of this species to three different environments: in a surface of compacted basalt, in pots and in troughs surrounded by water. In 'Une Idée' (An Idea, 1998) , French artist Liliana Motta, observing Chaumont's preference for recycled materials, created columns of plastic bottles empaled on concrete reinforcement rods. Filled with water (sometimes coloured) these striking constructions irrigated a luxuriant collection of polygonums.

Many blends exist between the two extremes of meadow and minimal. Each artist finds a different solution to the problem of ordering elements in space in a way which balances variety with clarity. In 2000, an intriguing garden called 'Traces, libertés d'aurore' (Traces, Dawn Liberties) was created by an artist, a garden designer and celebrated plantswoman Martine Lemonnier, who holds the French national collections of hellebore and meconopsis. Outlined like a leaf, this design alternated ribs of blue glass and pebbles with rich plantings enclosed by glass panels which bore ancient graphic symbols. Careful detailing successfully mingled with strong graphics.

One of the main attractions of the bedding plant theme of 2001 was its self-imposed geometrical framework which set fine fragments inside bolder structures. When combined as it often was with topiary, it readily mixed carpets and towers as horizontals and verticals – a form of 'living sculpture' both traditional and avant-garde. Participating designers did not experience the theme as a return to 19th-century city-park gardening. For one thing, the older version was merely a spectator sport, whereas Festival participants used great ingenuity to multiply angles of vision which engaged visitors more closely.

Where plant luxuriance holds sensuous appeal, conceptual compositions may seem cold. Designers, however, find games with abstract form – including language – seductive in their own right. Distinguished Swiss architect Dieter Kienast, the son of professional horticulturalists, insisted that always 'the exterior space must be a sensual place'.[5] His highly intellectual creation at Chaumont (1996) consisted of the sentence *Nature n'existe pas* (Nature does not exist) written in dwarf box on a pale wooden rectangle. In much smaller letters, at the entrance, spelled out in wooden sticks, was a conflicting sentiment: *Hommage à la nature* (Homage to nature). This paradox invited meditation in a garden where texture and architecture played equal parts, though plant variety was…minimal.

Above Daniel Örtli working for the city of Lausanne used mirrors amid alternating strips of meadow and lawn to create different perspectives, at once visual and symbolic.

Right 'Traces, libertés d'aurore' was laid out in the shape of a leaf. Its team included Martine Lemonnier, a nursery owner who holds national collections of hellebores and meconopsis.

garden of grasses

jardin de graminées 1994 Bob Wilson, USA

The *New York Times* described Robert Wilson as 'a towering figure in the world of experimental theatre and an explorer in the uses of time and space onstage.'[6] Offstage also: witness his *14 Stations* first commissioned by the village of Oberammergau in southern Germany, in conjunction with the Passion Play of 2000, and exhibited in 2002 at Mass MoCa, Massachusetts. Shaker houses and furniture inspired much of that design, on which Wilson commented: 'I always work with a horizontal line, which stands for time, and a vertical line, which, for me, always means space…. Time and space are two crossing lines, a structure that forms the architecture of everything.'[7] When Jean-Paul Pigeat invited Wilson to Chaumont in 1994, the artist was at home with the creation of

forms, but hesitant about plants. Luckily, he could call on his friend Mark Rudkin, an American painter and garden designer who, like Wilson, worked with Martha Graham in the 1950s. In 1954 Graham sent Rudkin to Paris where he took root and helped design gardens at the Palais Royal, at Giverny and at the Franco-American museum of the Château de Blérancourt. His creations are famous for their refined plantsmanship and painterly colours.

One day, Pigeat and Rudkin met Wilson on a stage at the Paris Opera. Together they worked out the overall plan, Wilson inscribing a circle within the tulip shape of a Chaumont plot. On site, Rudkin and Eric Ossart determined the plantings. It might be said that Wilson provided the architecture, Rudkin the texture. The painter chose the soft tones of mixed grasses, so often associated with meadows. Here they became themselves architectural, first by their arrangement in space, later by their growth through time. The tallest grasses were planted around a circle

Right Trees surrounding the plot added their structure to the design and created various light patterns without hindering the movement and sound of wind.

Plantsmen Mark Rudkin and Eric Ossart were among the first designers to experiment with grasses in garden plantings.

Plant Selection

Arundo donax Giant reed
Lamarckia aurea Golden top
Miscanthus floridulus
Miscanthus sinensis Eulalia
Rhynchelytrum repens
   Ruby grass
Setaria palmifolia Palm grass
Sorghum bicolor Great millet
Zea mays Ornamental maize,
   (red and white varieties)

Above and right Wilson's website biography states that: 'Transcending theatrical convention, Wilson draws in other performance and graphic arts, which coalesce into an integrated tapestry of images and sounds.' Chaumont was Wilson's first garden.

in the centre, with the others descending in height towards the outer boundaries. At the very heart was a stone seat which, in homage to his friend, Wilson called 'Mark's Chair'.

The inner space developed an atmosphere of its own, jungle-like and humid, with filtered shade in ever-changing patterns, closing in as the months advanced. Indeed, Wilson first saw his work in June when the plants were only 4 inches (10 centimetres) high. He was horrified – the bones were there but still bare; however, by September the garden room was complete. 'Bob Wilson, charmed, spent almost an hour sitting on his stone chair,' writes Pigeat. 'He had discovered the importance of time in the making of gardens…'.[8]

'Mark's Chair' in the secret heart of the garden was made of rough stone, only the seat being polished. By the summer's end this space had become truly private.

jacqueline's garden

un jardin pour jacqueline 2001 Eva Demarelatrous, Michel and Geneviève Gallais, Michel Arnaud, France

Jacqueline's was a friendship garden. Eva Demarelatrous, textile artist and German teacher in western France, dedicated a tapestry to a deceased friend and colleague, Jacqueline Picault. Wanting to do more, she developed a Chaumont proposal on the same design with the collaboration of Michel Arnaud, artist and teacher in Aubusson, central France, and of Michel and Geneviève Gallais, recently awarded the title of Best Gardeners of France. Michel Gallais regularly holds workshops for the Chaumont Conservatoire and he and Geneviève are two of the five municipal gardeners working in the small town of Marans in western France. Geneviève comments, 'It is like a big family.'

Little by little, Eva's tapestry became a huge living mosaic where the Gallais's choice plants were enhanced by strong outlines and changing levels. Raised beds with undulating surfaces were planted with a refined palette of ground covers. Varied textures, foliage and flower colours were interspersed with other 'tactile experiences': carpets of stainless-steel scrubbing pads, strips of plastic and sisal doormats, pieces of wall-to-wall carpeting turned upside down, wedges of plastic bubble wrap, fragments of insulation materials and swathes of cobalt blue glass bubbles. Aluminium 'fins' rose here and there and from an aluminium arch overhead hung strings of transparent plastic balls, a 'crystal-beaded curtain' which dripped water onto the plants below.

An itinerary was carefully planned for contrasts. Demarelatrous made three vast curtains reproducing the original design to hang at the entrance, hiding the mysteries beyond. Once inside, visitors discovered the same design inverted, now horizontal and brightly coloured. Demarelatrous also imagined paths of

To provide vertical contrast, a giant 'bead' curtain repeated the undulating design while evoking the weaver's loom. It was also a watering device.

Opposite For the *mosaïculture* (carpet bedding) theme of 2001, two artists and two horticulturalists translated a fabric wall hanging into a horizontal plant tapestry. The pattern of the original wall hanging was reproduced on curtains at the entrance, which also hid the garden from the outside.

crushed brick and gravel leading into the garden, providing lively sound effects and colour contrasts. Inside the garden, however, quiet, black rubber paths wound through the mini-labyrinth, first sunken to provide immersion, then rising to afford a general view. Many easily accessible plants – mint, thyme, basil – released rich scents when lightly brushed in passing. The overall effect was first disorientation, then discovery and enjoyment.

'Un Jardin pour Jacqueline' was a dynamic reworking of the static bedding theme. Strongly defined structures framed a richly textured range of plants and materials. It was horticulturally varied and technically ingenious. Each collaborator contributed an essential part and, as a result, the four have become fast friends.

A particularly rich range of ground cover plants grew amid patches of stainless-steel scrubbing pads, plastic doormats, wall-to-wall carpeting placed upside down, plastic bubble wrap, coconut doormats and insulation materials.

Plants undulated in their own way by sinking, dipping and rising along a defined itinerary. Visitors were directed by the design itself as soon as they passed the magic curtains.

Plant Selection

Acorus gramineus 'Ogon'
  Slender sweet flag
Alternanthera bettzichiana
  'Brilliantissima' Calico plant
Artemisia alba 'Canescens'
Artemisia schmidtiana 'Nana'
Begoniax tuberhybrida
  'Non Stop' Hybrid begonia
Beta vulgaris 'Mac Gregor's
  Favorite' Beet
Calocephalus brownii
Carex buchananii
  Leatherleaf sedge
Carex hachijoensis 'Evergold'
Coreopsis verticillata 'Zagreb'
Cotula hispida
Diascia barberiae 'Ruby Field'
Erigeron glaucus Aster
Gazania rigens 'Chansonnette'
  Treasure flower
Helichrysum petiolare
  'Limelight' ('Aurea')
  Liquorice plant
Hosta x tardiana 'Halcyon'
Hypoestes phyllostachya
  'Confetti' Polka-dot plant
Imperata cylindrica 'Red
  Baron' ('Rubra') Chigaya
Iresine herbstii 'Brilliantissima'
  Beefsteak plant
Lamium maculatum
  'White Nancy' Dead nettle
Lamium maculatum 'Aureum'
Lysimachia nummularia
  'Aurea' Creeping Jenny
Mentha suaveolens variegata
  Apple mint
Milium effusum 'Aureum'
  Wood millet
Ocimum basilicum
  'Purpureum' Purple basil
Ophiopogon japonicus
  'Major'
Ophiopogon planiscapus
  'Nigrescens'
Pereskia aculeata
  'Godseffiana'
Pilea microphylla
Santolina rosmarinifolia
  Holy Flax
Sanvitalia procumbens
  'Sprite'
Solenostemon scutellarioides
  Wizard 'Sunset' Coleus
Stenotaphrum secundatum
  St Augustine grass
Tanacetum parthenium
  'Aureum' and 'Golden
  Moss' Golden feverfew
Thymus pseudolanuginosus
  Woolly thyme

Michel and Geneviève Gallais have been 'accompanying'
Chaumont gardens since the Festival's inception. Their work as
municipal gardeners in a small town bears witness to Chaumont's
wide impact.

outdoor art

The historian John Dixon Hunt proposes the term 'exterior place-making' to embrace landscape architecture, garden design and land, nature or earth art. Garden festivals also fit this definition. For although their creations are often dismissed as temporary outdoor installations, they share the ambition that Hunt attributes to all landscape architecture, the desire to 're-present land as art'. The debate over their legitimacy often turns on the rapport between man-made constructs and growing plants – what many have viewed in a larger context as 'culture' versus 'nature'. American landscape architects have often cited Wallace Stevens's poem 'Anecdote of the Jar' in this regard, though Stevens's image is cunningly ambiguous: 'I placed a jar in Tennessee / And round it was, upon a hill / It made the slovenly wilderness / Surround that hill.'[1] The formal artifact appears to conquer nature: 'It took dominion everywhere'. This is the phrase that some historians apply to André Le Nôtre's work in France. Some of his spiritual descendants link geometry to artifice and art, judging nature's lines to be, if not 'slovenly', at least biomorphic. In 1991, the earth artist Richard Long wrote, 'You could say that my work is a balance between the patterns of nature and the formalism of human, abstract ideas like lines and circles.'[2] At Chaumont James Wines of the SITE agency, an architecture and environmental arts group, created 'Entre Géométrie et nature libre' (Between Geometry and Free Nature, 1992). Here the linearity of 'Art' was set against the exuberance of 'Nature'.

The American landscape architects Peter Walker and Martha Schwartz have each spent years exploring connections between painting and landscape architecture. Sometimes in their works the whole landscape becomes 'jar' – site geometries dominate organic elements altogether. In a festival context, the equivalent is an 'installation' where construction eliminates plants. Thus, 'Ciné Mosaïc' (Mosaic Flicks, 2001), presenting white artificial flowers in a black tent lit by an overhead projector, provoked protests that this was not a garden.

In recent years, another view of the art/nature relationship has held sway, in which both are inventions of human 'culture'. Richard Weller, describing his collaboration with Vladimir Sitta, offers a postmodern interpretation: 'The "nature" which landscape architects often have in mind is only a nostalgic surface image of landscape, a culturally specific selection…. We suffer no illusion that culture is to be redeemed by a pure nature or vice versa. We are operating in the domain of the de-natured.'[3] Writers as diverse as Michael Pollan, Augustin Berque and Simon Schama all agree that 'culture' is simply part of our own human nature, a way of perceiving that defines our species and includes landscape. Schama writes: 'Landscapes are constructs of the imagination projected onto wood and water and rock.' They become a form of outdoor art, whatever their size, situation or duration.

Garden historians acknowledge that the most apparently 'natural' creations have always required the most artful intervention, from Capability Brown's earthworks to today's meadows or James Wines's garden at Chaumont. Geometries clearly exist everywhere in nature. Among practising landscape architects, Roberto Burle Marx appears once more as a pioneer. An abstract painter as well as landscape architect, he created gardens that were both exuberantly alive and formally patterned. International garden festivals, where temporary installations mix growing and inorganic materials in varying proportions and combinations, could provide the ideal place for experiments on these themes. Dieter Kienast's statements: 'Homage to Nature' and 'Nature does not exist' are perhaps not really so contradictory after all.

Opposite above Plants such as agaves make strong statements as sculptures in their own right, especially when used in unexpected contexts.

Right Sometimes at Chaumont, objects dominate by rising in clouds high above the hedging ('Ombres et Ombelles' 1996).

Opposite below Small floating baskets of vegetables become kinetic sculpture in 'Le Potager dansant' (The Dancing Potager, 1998).

structures and sculptures

'Trajectoire' (Trajectory, 1999) created a miniature landscape with a camomile river running through lettuce valleys. An arch supporting pumpkins overhead was suggestive of the sun's course.

Many of Chaumont's exhibits consist of a stunning focal point surrounded by informal vegetation: a sculpture or a water device rising from the plantings such as Stevens's jar on the hill. Often the object provides a necessary vertical presence in a treeless plot. The challenge here is to engage with the site – even in the immediate, limited context of a festival plot. The American landscape architect Robert Irwin established a four-part typology in this regard: works that dominate the site, those that are adjusted to its scale though brought in from elsewhere, those that are wholly site-specific and those that are so determined by the site that they are inseparable from the earth, involving its very elements.[4]

Stevens's jar was eminently transportable – indeed it seems it was a bootlegger's whisky jar! Once judiciously placed, however, it changed everything, affecting not so much the place itself as the viewer's perception of it. A more random siting might have produced mere juxtaposition, as with old-fashioned outdoor sculpture museums, which simply set artworks down in an agreeably neutral setting. The Festival equivalent is an elaborate construct surrounded by a pleasant green and floral decor.

Some artists at Chaumont multiply structures that rise high above the hedging, grouped in seemingly random order, and so striking that they alone 'stand out' in the design. Memorable examples include black umbrellas on poles in 'Ombres et Ombelles' (Umbrage and Umbels, 1996), the floating red plastic chairs representing flood destruction in the Canadian creation 'Le Déluge' (The Deluge, 1998) or the plumed hatpins of 'Entre Epingles' (Among Hatpins, 2001). The effect is stunning, though internal coherence may suffer and neighbours usually mind.

Garden art has its own clever structures which integrate rather than dominate plantings: pergolas and pots. Both have been much exploited in Chaumont festival designs. Containers became powerful verticals in Michel Desvigne and Christine Dalnoky's 'Tontines' or 'Panier' (Basket, 1994) a display of the baskets traditionally used by the great plant hunters to transport plants over long distances. A more permanent version of this composition by the same designers now graces a courtyard at Charles de Gaulle airport, Terminal Three.

Large mirrors may also pull a composition together. Robert Smithson used them horizontally in such a way that they were 'hidden' in the landscape, making it impossible to distinguish reality from reflection. Artists at Chaumont tend to make them stand clear, neither immersed nor irrevocably rooted, perhaps because of the intimate nature of the festival genre or because of the general need in these plots to introduce verticals. One example using mirrors at Chaumont was in fact named the 'Jardin de l'artifice naturel et de la nature artificielle' (Garden of Natural Artifice and Artificial Nature, 1994).

Today outdoor-art museums often commission works inseparable from their site. A garden festival by its very nature encourages this approach. Actual earthworks are harder to create in festival conditions, but 'Trajectoire' (Trajectory, 1999) managed a miniature landscape of parsley-carpeted hills surrounded by a camomile river. Such an installation is not only alive, it also evolves over the summer. Time and growth become part of its theme, bringing it closer to the traditional garden mode.

Above and right The vibrant 'Ailleurs' (Elsewhere, 1996), created by two students from the Ecole Boulle, stretched bright pink canvas in waves close to the ground. This installation was closely welded to its site with only cacti, agaves and yuccas emerging. The plants and structures, like the colours, were complementary.

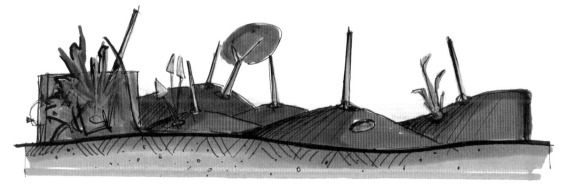

the gloriette

Fernando Caruncho 1993 Spain

The Spanish designer Fernando Caruncho is known for his elegant but earthy mastery of formal geometries. Though linked to contemporary minimalism, his approach has deep roots in ancient Greek and Arab metaphysics. Historians have sometimes associated the Mediterranean love of forms, both intellectual and material, to the sculptural quality of southern light. As Caruncho explains, 'I strive to arrange a space that invites reflection and inquiry by allowing the light to delineate geometries, and this way discover the dynamic symmetries of nature.'[5] He has no patience with the misty sentimentality of Rousseau or the nostalgic clutter of English 'granny gardens'. His great models are the Alhambra, Vaux-le-Vicomte, the Boboli gardens in Florence, Russell Page and Luís Barragan.

Similarly Mediterranean is Caruncho's evocation of agricultural geometries: not merely a personal trait, Caruncho's use of wheat fields and vineyards continues a southern tradition which never completely separated ornamental and productive gardening, pleasure and profit. Much of his work involves a generous sense of scale with views on to surrounding landscapes.

How could a plot at Chaumont covering merely 2,690 square feet (250 square metres) in a climate famous for its moist and variable luminosity, allow scope for such a vision? The space allotted to Fernando Caruncho in 1992 did offer a dramatic view of Chaumont's Renaissance towers and the designer chose to build a long wooden arbour facing them. In the middle ground, only the simplest shapes and plantings were suitable. The plot's central axis was extended into a square with projections on three sides, using a frame with the same rough wood as the arbour. Slightly raised, it also 'corrected' the

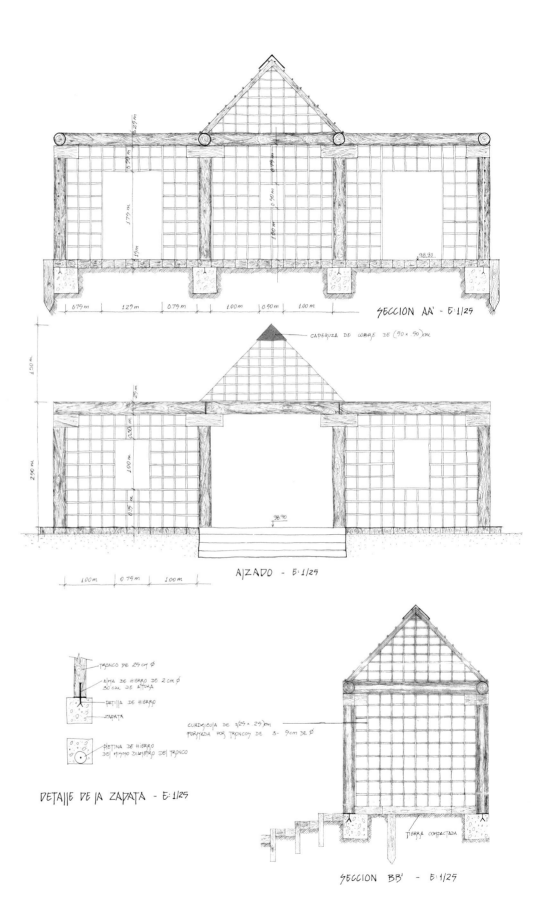

steep slope, creating a gently unfolding panorama of the château beyond. The proportions were perfect, the series of planes both gentle and controlled. The square was planted in blue and gold, using summer blooming *Salvia farinacea* 'Victoria' and *Dahlia* 'München'. Why did the designer allow floral colour in this composition, which he reduces elsewhere to a minimum? It was surely in response to the light of the Loire valley as well as a way of providing textural contrast. Colourful bedding also suits the cultural context of the châteaux and summer festivals of the Loire valley.

Caruncho's work is characterized not only by geometry, but also by 'shaving shape and telling texture'.[6] The elegant wooden structure was made of rough-hewn logs with the bark still on. In 1993 the theme had changed to 'Imagination during Recession', but this structure remained and exemplified the use of simple, inexpensive materials. Thus, the essential elements of Caruncho's style were all contained here in miniature: symmetry, concision, harmony with the surroundings, a meditation on the quality of light, rustic allusion (in the materials used) and a traditional formality leaning towards modern minimalism.

Opposite and right Fernando Caruncho has designed gardens all over Spain, in the USA and the south of France and is currently creating a garden for the Spanish embassy in Tokyo. Caruncho's elegant balance between ancient Mediterranean models and minimalist forms has made him a leader in contemporary design.

does the mint lie?

mente la menta? 2000 Marco Antonini, Roberto Capecci
and Raffaella Sini, Italy

The Land-I agency based in Rome consists of three
landscape architects who have created ingenious
temporary gardens for festivals in Italy, Berlin and
in 2002, for the 'Jardin des Métis' in Quebec. Their
installation at Chaumont, 'Mente la menta?', won
the Luigi Piccinato prize from the Ordine degli
Architetti di Roma, and was admired in *Le Monde*
newspaper as *très chic*. This it certainly was, but it
was much more as well. A seamless combination
of sculpture and earth art, it contained only one
species of plant: aquatic mint. But this single green
presence, fragrant and powerfully proliferating,
was the key to the whole work.

Four elements met here: 'the Void, the Raft,
Smoke and Nature'. These in turn represented,
according to the creators, our unknown future
in the new millennium, the uncertain platform on
which man floats, the complexity and shadows
of our contemporary world, and nature's capacity
for survival. Hence the title 'Does The Mint Lie?'.
Can we believe nature's promise for the future?
'Mente la menta?' is also a pun on the noun *mente*,
meaning 'mind', and on *la menta* for the verb 'lament'.
A second translation would then be 'does the mind
suffer?'. The Land-I team described its work as
involving not only 'the land as a medium of expression',
but also the 'act of observing and interpreting'.

Even visitors who did not fully grasp this
conceptual complexity responded to its material
translation. The void was a round pool containing
floating pieces of black charcoal which kept the
water pure, but also recalled the ominous threat
of black tides. Around the pool a circular deck made
of pine planks resembled a floating raft, though in

Land-I's work explores the complex relationships between man and
space in ways which are powerful both conceptually and physically.

Opposite above Older land and earth art concentrated on decay.
Today, artists explore growth, here in the mint but also in the
vegetation surrounding the Festival plot.

Opposite below The steel wool and wire 'smoke' beautifully caught
light and shadow while suggesting both passage
and enclosure.

fact it was securely anchored. Jutting out over the water, it allowed human beings to penetrate the symbolic landscape. The most spectacular element was the smoke: undulating 'cushions' of twisted wire netting, the more opaque ones covered with steel wool, alternating darkness and light, here peaking, there subsiding. Silhouetted against the dark clipped greenery of the surrounding hedge, the wire structures exerted a forceful attraction, not least because of the thousand mint shoots, thrusting through them as the summer progressed.

The project was conceived with the help of the architects Gianna Attiani and Daniela Mongini. For the Land-I team, the union of nature, sculpture and architecture, like the link between matter and mental activity, represents the way forward, part of the optimism symbolized here by the mint's inexorable growth.

moving designs

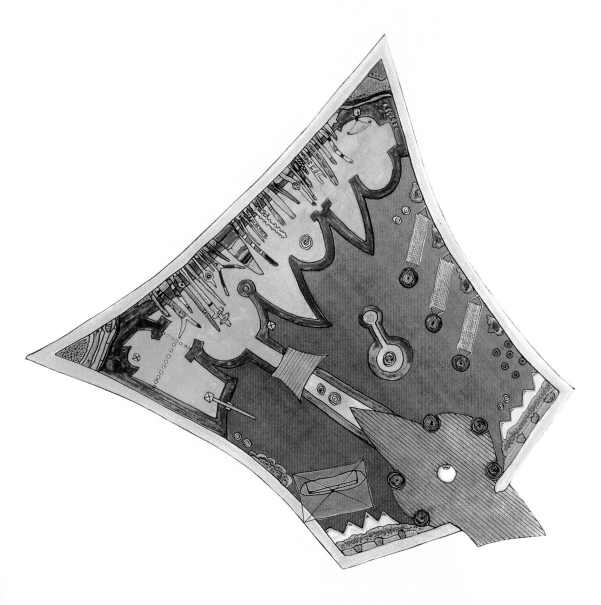

The 'Ricochet' theme of 1998 suggested moving water. 'Ricochets sur l'art de vivre' used driftwood water jets in a siesta setting to create gurgles, gentle hissing, rustling, whistling, lapping and bubbling.

'Artists today,' writes the French critic Gilles A. Tiberghien, 'are more interested in process than objects.' Gardens offer special opportunities for kinetic sculpture, as they are usually full of moving elements. Today many private gardens are either designed to attract wildlife or include aviaries. Wind may also create motion and in 'L'Eolienne' (The Windpump, 1998) Jean Lautrey went so far as to install a rickety windpump, though he chose the ironic mode of rusty metal rising from a carpet of scraggly lysimachia. In 'Ricochets' (1998), large pebbles on rods rose from strips of statice, artemesia and pennisetum, colliding when the wind blew. There are also designs which seem to be in movement: a ribbon snakes its way around the plot, much like the unwinding filmstrip that determined the outlines of the Villette Park in Paris ('Rubans', Ribbons, 2001).

Water is perhaps the most common source of movement in garden design. One popular exhibit was the 'Potager dansant' (Dancing Potager, 1998), in which small baskets of vegetables floated on water and regularly bumped into each other, a 'new way of tossing salads!' wrote Jean-Paul Pigeat. A feature at Chaumont for many years was a great waterwheel, the Noria, first built as a musical device but then incorporated into successive gardens as a moving sculpture. In 'Main Coulante' (Flowing Handrail, 2000–2002), water flowed down an iron handrail which had been transformed into a canal. Misting or fog devices add motion to many gardens that would otherwise be solid.

Movement in garden design is often experienced as seasonal change, or through the creation of sound effects (see Chapter 4). It also becomes a kind of performance when visitors are directly involved – children getting soaked in the Pro Urba jungle or visitors cranking up parts in the 'Le Carrousel d'eau' (The Water Carousel, see p. 90). In 2001 a group of German designers made movement the theme of their creation: metal containers on wheels were rearranged at will by visitors forming geometric patterns. Thus, visitors were able to enter into the creative process as into the space of the work.

Right The water wheel or 'Noria' was created to set in motion the first 'Orgue hydraulique' (Hydraulic Organ) in 1997. It later contributed to other gardens such as the 'Vol de canards' (Flight of Ducks, 2001).

Below Claudia Cheikh-Gonzalez and Isabelle Ropelato imagined pebbles blowing on wires among stripes of Mediterranean plants above the Loire's flow ('Ricochets' 1998).

nature's code

code naturel 2000 pep Studio: Katharina Schütze, Uwe Müller and Jürgen Stellwag, Germany

The pep Studio from Berlin designed a giant shimmering mobile to juxtapose two types of knowledge. On the one hand, our traditional perception of plants, symbolized by a lush garden richly furnished with cottagey flowers such as Madonna lilies, campanula, buddleia and lupins; on the other, the computerized transformation of plants into digital codes – language rather than matter – was expressed as trellissed screens of hanging laser discs. Thus, the old opposition between nature and artifice was restated and updated: irregular, curving lines and sloping ground surrounded squared-off, patterned uprights. From the latter hung some 4,500 compact discs, screwed together in pairs for equal brilliance on both sides and strung from structures of nylon wire, steel cables and copper piping. Reflections moved in both directions: the discs shedding colour on the mainly white and blue blossoms while picking up darting light from their surroundings as they moved. Red exclamation marks were provided here and there by scarlet runner beans. The floral exuberance, together with these floating geometries, created multiple and shifting viewpoints.

The key figure in this enigma was in fact the visitor whose presence was also symbolic: any human being – another moving element in the design – represents the species that can choose to protect, eliminate or change plant life. 'Natural' or digital, the modulations of the future are ours to determine.

Katharina Schütze remembers that 'the path of white broken glass in the centre of the installation was shimmering a little blue as well and gave a very special sensation while walking through.' Another

'Code naturel' centred on the visitors' changing vision from both outside and inside the labyrinth. Scintillating curtains bore mysterious information while reflecting off living plants.

path meant to resemble a river bed was surfaced with pebbles from the Loire river. The pep Studio generally incorporates references to context in its installations, even inner-city works containing no plants at all. Two of their group trained as landscape architects and one as an architect, but today all work as artists. They often exploit everyday objects to 'deconstruct habits and generate new sensory experiences'. Working either individually or together, they also team up with other specialists, such as the architect Thomas Büsch who worked closely with the pep team at Chaumont. Katharina recalls the time spent preparing their Festival project as enormously inspirational: 'Today I am thinking of Chaumont every once in a while and it seems to me that I am still deriving energy from this time.'

Right Man-manipulated structures contrasted tellingly with cottagey plants such as Japanese anenomes, asters, echinops, catanche, felicia, eryngium, festuca, thyme, catnip, daisies, 'Iceberg' roses and buddleia.

Opposite Common to all elements – the most artificial and the most natural – was the importance of light and reflection, symbolic as well as physical.

the water carousel

le carrousel d'eau 1997 Michèle Elsaïr and Jean-Pierre
Delettre, France

The architect Michèle Elsaïr and the inventor Jean-
Pierre Delettre imagined an amazing structure
displaying the reflections and motion of water.
A shallow pool of 1,075 square feet (100 square
metres) was painted black to resemble a silted
country pond where the tall trees mirrored in the
water seemed to plumb immeasurable depths.
A wall of large-leafed plants, Indian rhubarb (*Darmera
peltata*) and giant butterbur (*Petasites japonicus*)
encroached on the water 'like a hem,' says Elsaïr.
Within the pool, five parallel strips contrasted five
types of movement. When visitors turned a crank,
the broadest strip freed bubbles among floating
water lettuce. The next strip used a hidden blade
fan to create gentle ripples around a still rectangle
of duckweed. The third broke up reflections with
stronger air currents from opposite sides, around
a mosaic of fairy moss (*Azolla caroliniana*) and water
chestnut (*Trapa natans*). The fourth contained a plant
ferry which conveyed a small stand of horsetail back
and forth, leaving ripples in its wake. In the fifth and
narrowest strip, water dripping from fishing rods
created endless, rhythmic circles around another
rectangle of duckweed.

Colours were soft and natural except for the
tall red masts of spiralled braces, rising 23 feet
(7 metres) high on either side. These provided volume
and height, but also cast their own diagonal shadows
across the parallel lines. Visitors could look down
from the wooden and metal staircase rising along one
side, and from the top they could glimpse the ever-
changing Loire river in the distance. The variations
on movement and reflection were infinite according
to season and time of day, weather and mood.

Variations on moving water were illustrated by this fantastic structure
which invited visitor participation.

Opposite above 'Le Carrousel d'eau' is once again a creation that
balances plants with innovative technology. Butterburs, ligularias,
hostas, duckweeds, water lettuces and water hyacinths surrounded
the carousel itself.

Opposite below The idea of 'plant ferries' caused much amusement,
and not just for the many children who visited Chaumont. 'Le
Carrousel d'eau' beautifully incorporated the performance aspect
of kinetic sculpture.

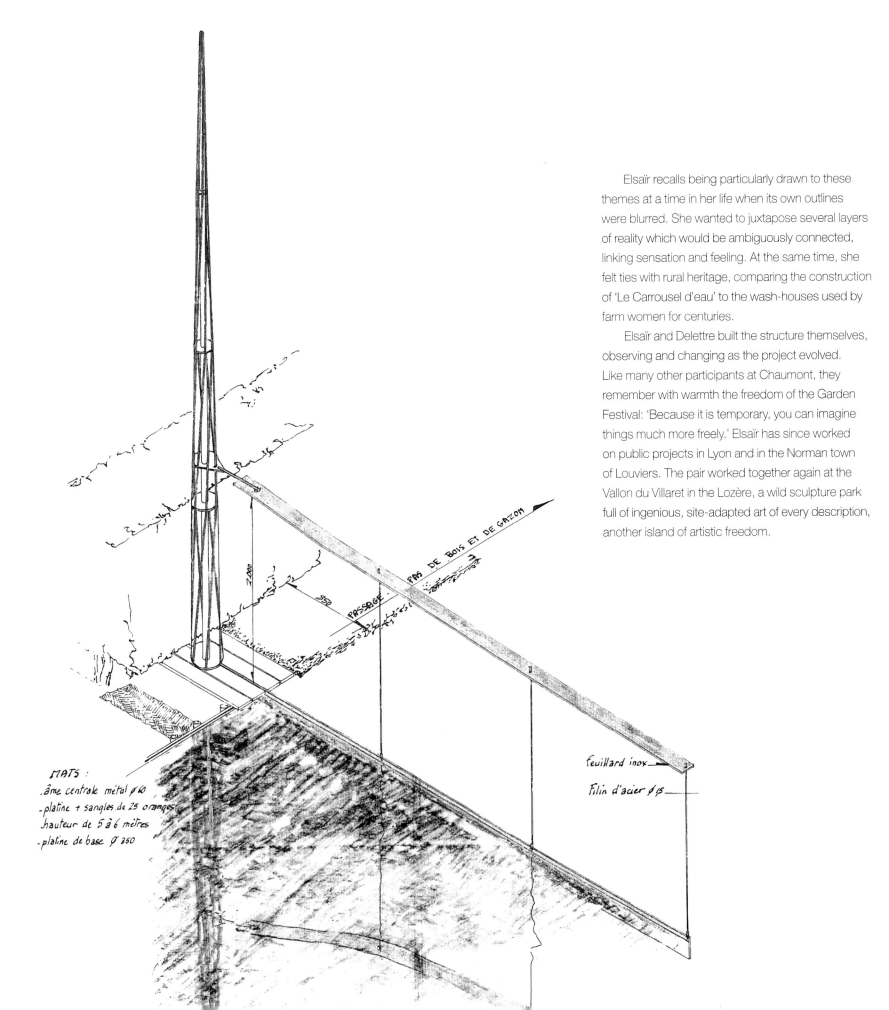

Elsaïr recalls being particularly drawn to these themes at a time in her life when its own outlines were blurred. She wanted to juxtapose several layers of reality which would be ambiguously connected, linking sensation and feeling. At the same time, she felt ties with rural heritage, comparing the construction of 'Le Carrousel d'eau' to the wash-houses used by farm women for centuries.

Elsaïr and Delettre built the structure themselves, observing and changing as the project evolved. Like many other participants at Chaumont, they remember with warmth the freedom of the Garden Festival: 'Because it is temporary, you can imagine things much more freely.' Elsaïr has since worked on public projects in Lyon and in the Norman town of Louviers. The pair worked together again at the Vallon du Villaret in the Lozère, a wild sculpture park full of ingenious, site-adapted art of every description, another island of artistic freedom.

PAS DE BOIS ET DE GAZON

PASSAGE

MATS :
- âme centrale métal ∅ 40
- platine + sangles de 25 oranges
- hauteur de 5 à 6 mètres
- platine de base ∅ 350

feuillard inox

Filin d'acier ∅ 5

'Le Caroussel d'eau' felt self-contained but in fact maintained subtle links with the physical setting of the Chaumont plot, while drawing on familiar woodland associations.

Left Reflections changed constantly from second to second. The effect of such motion could be mesmerizing, leading to a feeling of stillness in the viewer.

inside stories

During the Renaissance, Western garden art became a projection of architecture, an extension of the lines and volumes of the building it surrounded. In the late 18th century, painting became a major model, implying a spectacle with a series of managed viewpoints. Today, the conventional boundaries separating architecture and sculpture from landscape architecture are blurred. As Tiberghien comments, designers 'think more in terms of space than images.' There are multiple angles of vision – including those from inside.

Most of the plots at Chaumont invite visitors to enter. Layouts are rarely readable from the entrance and itineraries moving round the spaces, however small, change as you advance. One of the most wonderful examples was the 'Tunnel de bambous' (Bamboo Tunnel) of the Japanese film-maker Hiroshi Teshigahara. Over the years, the plantings became so dense that it had to be removed, but the experience it offered of light and shade, of mystery and discovery, was quite unforgettable.

There have been other tunnels, some raised, some sunken, some on ground level – 'L'Arche de Noé' (Noah's Ark, 1997) with its raised 'library' of plants, or the tunnels of the mould garden (see p. 166). These works bend garden design towards the narrative pattern of initiatory travel (see Chapter 4), since 'entering in' always means crossing a boundary to explore a separate world of fantasy. Many gardens exploring the 2002 theme of eroticism played on entry and initiation, creating seductive labyrinths and enticing gateways.

Indoor and outdoor spaces interconnect in unpredictable ways. One garden deliberately inversed them, spoofing the idea of the 'outdoor room' by providing yellow lampshades on the watering spouts and creating furniture from plant 'pouffes'. The Australian Jenny Jones imagined 'Un Jardin ne peut avoir d'existence sans nous' (A Garden Cannot Exist

Without Us, 2000). A long glass table offered plants like tantalizing food for guests. Jones wrote, 'When we picture a garden we should be in the picture too!'

There have also been gardens that keep visitors outside and impose a single angle of vision, like stage sets – many of the exhibiting artists are scenographers, after all. 'Le Théâtre d'eau' (The Water Theatre, 1997) was a series of parallel canals around vegetable beds, with a bench at one end for viewing the changing light and seasonal growth. The sense of peace and enclosure attenuated theatrical distance. Sometimes, a viewing platform was provided to see exhibits from above, usually a raised bridge, like the blue polished glass suspended over a sea of lavender which was created by the Quasar Institute from Rome. And true to the American land art tradition, some gardens are best perceived through aerial photography, George Hargreaves's garden 'La Terre en marche' (The Earth in Motion) among them (see p. 144). More typical of Chaumont was the 'Potager en L'île' (Island Potager, 1994). All along the edge of the pool were water sprayers with which visitors could cool off by spraying themselves or each other, and pumps for making bubbles in the water.

'Where is the fine line between performance, installation and garden design?' Jane Amidon asks in *Radical Landscapes*, concluding: 'Perhaps it is best to permit ambiguity to breed richness of interpretation.'

Left and opposite below Writing about 'Un Jardin ne peut pas exister sans nous', Jenny Jones invited visitors to 'celebrate a supper of plenty, rich in flavour, ripe and colourful, the flowering of our lifelong relationship with nature.'

Opposite above 'Potager en l'île' (Island Potager) floated islands of exotic plants to be admired, but also touched and smelled. The water was heated by an army of glass bottles.

straw hut garden

jardin de paille 2000 Hugues Peuvergne, France

Hugues Peuvergne became a gardener so he could live and work outdoors. He does not separate design and upkeep, considering that, like children, gardens need care after birth. Childhood is in fact a constant inspiration for him. His straw garden at Chaumont resembled a huge playhouse, bird's nest and medieval stronghold all at once. Haystacks in fields first gave him the idea of constructing this space like a set of dominoes: 120 bales of straw, each weighing 250 kilogrammes, were assembled with 8 cubic metres of earth and held together with metal rods and woven linden fences. Little by little, plants set out on three platforms consolidated the structure. Peuvergne chose only familiar varieties: buddleias and false valerian, California poppies, dill and fennel, jasmin and honeysuckle, lilac, mock orange and the rose 'Ghislaine de Féligonde'.

Entering this space meant negotiating a labyrinth that prevented any exterior views until unexpectedly, about half way up, you reached a belvedere. A true Romantic, Peuvergne wanted visitors to feel they were the first to penetrate this magic space, but then to discover traces of 'the gardener within' – an alarm clock, a mirror, a vase of wild flowers. People felt welcome and many ate their picnics here. A mailbox invited comments. Children were overheard to wonder if this was the cabin of the Three Little Pigs of the fairy tale and adults reminisced about their grandparents' farm.

Peuvergne did most of the work himself, even during the summer season, for the garden evolved: climbers infiltrated unexpected places and the straw deteriorated in unpredicted ways. Some parts were thus more picturesque in September than in June –

Above and left Seemingly naïve and childlike, Peuvergne's garden played cleverly with transitions and changing viewpoints. Trees emerged here and there from the dense, but unintimidating battlements: a *Gleditsia triacanthos* 'Sunburst' and an ornamental apple tree (*Malus* 'Everest').

Opposite Inspired by the assemblages of common haystacks in fields, Peuvergne's creation blurred distinctions between outdoor and indoor spaces by burrowing within the object itself.

During the Chaumont season, Peuvergne came every two weeks
to inspect his creation, noting with pleasure the unexpected evolution
of plants like the Virginia creeper.

though always subject to security checks. The garden, says Peuvergne, 'had its own life. You had to keep an eye on it all the time. But I love being surprised by my garden.'

As a result of this exhibit, Peuvergne was invited to build tree houses near Cézanne's former studio in Aix-en-Provence, a fairy-tale fantasy intended to last for three years. Tiberghien writes about the current fashion for *cabanes* that 'they are the ideal meeting place of art and nature, echoing the origins of art and civilization, the evolution of the species as of the individual.' Peuvergne might not claim so much, but there is no doubt that for him art is an immersion in nature.

Below and right Peuvergne's straw hut was an early example of the fashion for tree houses and children's play huts of all kinds, found today even in hotel gardens. Few exhibits have made visitors feel as welcome, children as well as adults, which is in keeping with Chaumont's desire to cater for youngsters.

woven willows

saules tressées 1995–96 David and Judy Drew, England

David and Judy Drew have been living in central France since the early 1990s. Their village, Villaines-les-Rochers, lives from basket weaving, housing a successful craft cooperative of eighty families as well as independent artists. David Drew is a star among them: internationally known for over thirty years, he constituted a collection of willows useful for his art

which is now in the care of the Royal Botanic Gardens at Kew, London. Judy Drew taught fine art in England in earlier days, but in the last two decades the two have developed a unique medium which she defines as 'a mixture between land art, building and installations'. Since the 1995 Chaumont Festival, new projects have included a boathouse for Mick Jagger and an installation at the Rockefeller Center in New York.

The Drews created their live willow fencing at Chaumont in 1995. This technique has since entered French garden culture, even in the popular magazines.

For 'Woven Willows', Jean-Paul Pigeat agreed to remove
the hedging that normally surrounds each plot so that distant
perspectives could be possible.

The live willow design was meant to be experienced from all angles, inside and out. Children loved playing hide-and-seek in its meanders.

Their Chaumont experience began when Jean-Paul Pigeat personally invited them to come. Judy remembers that David had recently fallen off a ladder and lacked enthusiasm, but Pigeat insisted. And so, she recounts, they left their troglodyte house and large vegetable garden and went to Chaumont where 'in late February, early March, we planted the three-metre-high willows ("Noire de Villaines" variety). Leaves appeared a few weeks later, and it was soon well covered with foliage.' At planting, the stems were woven into the diamond pattern that David had invented in Somerset in 1982. The layout was intricate and simple all at once, both minimalist-modern and reminiscent of ancient civilizations. Ivory-coloured sand was spread on the paths to emphasize shadows, and grass was seeded outside between the 'ribs'.

For the first time at Chaumont, Pigeat agreed to remove the hedge so that the entire structure could stand free and be seen from afar as well as within. For this was very much a work to explore from every angle, inside and out. As the season progressed and shoots grew, it stirred more with the wind. Visitors could be glimpsed through the tracery, providing the main movement and colour, especially children playing hide-and-seek in the mini-labyrinth, which they loved to do.

This was very much a site-specific installation involving growing plants. It lasted four seasons and, had it remained, would have evolved into a completely grafted structure. Few gardens at Chaumont have been so widely copied, from home gardens to traffic roundabouts, all over France and beyond. Drastically pruned in the autumn, it was kept on in 1997 when the Chaumont team added regular spurts of ground mist to transform it into a new exhibit, 'Saules dans la brume' (Willows in the Mist).

Above 'Woven Willows' is another example of 'nature art' which incorporates the energies of living plant growth to create spaces which evolve through time.

Left The basic design for the willow plantings was simple and supple, like the plant used. It evokes ancient crafts and modern minimalism all at once.

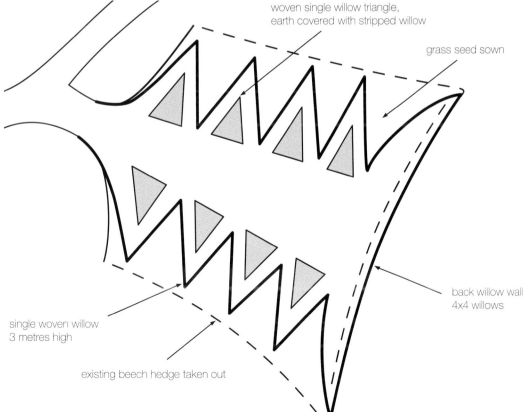

woven single willow triangle,
earth covered with stripped willow

grass seed sown

back willow wall
4x4 willows

single woven willow
3 metres high

existing beech hedge taken out

4

time and change

The land artist Walter de Maria once wrote: 'The artist who works with earth, works with time.'[1] Home gardeners of course confront time and change daily, struggling to grow huge tomato vines from tiny seeds, or to associate perennials so they bloom together year after year. Land artists avoided plants precisely because, as Udo Weilacher comments in his history of the movement, 'The living plant often develops an unpredictable momentum of its own and actively alters its environment.' In 1968 Robert Smithson went so far as to ask: 'Could one say that art degenerates as it approaches gardening?'[2] Smithson was fascinated with process but preferred decay to growth. Gardeners consider decay a condition of growth and their model is compost – the past recycled, death giving life.

Today, with the convergence of art and garden design, more and more place-makers include living materials. Landscape architects Michel Courajoud, Richard Haag and Jacques Wirtz all work with nature as a dynamic process evolving over years and incorporating both seasonal change and long-term growth. Haag and Wirtz began their careers as nurserymen. Roberto Burle Marx, who started his career as a painter, nonetheless revelled in 'living, mutating raw material'. Gilles Clément offers an even more energetic exploration of growth and change. His *jardin en mouvement* (moving garden) is based on watching the evolution of spontaneous vegetation so that he may intervene at its point of greatest diversity.[3] Who but Clément would compare landscape architecture to jumping on the back of a running horse?

John Dixon Hunt reminds us that dance and body painting alone resemble garden design 'as arts that actively involve a living, organic and changing component'. His comparison implies the fleeting energy of a performance, the passing moment captured as art. The British horticulturalist Hugh Johnson, while agreeing that true gardeners love 'the slow ripening of the seasons and the gradual maturing of a cherished plan', nonetheless dared to ask: 'If change is a significant part of gardening pleasure, why should one insist (or even prefer) that it happen slowly?' He sees gardens as process at whatever speed.[4] Place-makers today experience time more and more dynamically – even instantaneously. The British nature artists Richard Long and Andy Goldsworthy were among the first to explore this vein, the latter's frost and rain shadows lasting merely seconds. In France, Eric Ossart and Arnaud Maurières, working with students, have created numerous short-lived gardens. 'Permanence is not reasonable,' they write. 'The gardener is master of the ephemeral. Only some trees and the soil that bears them seem eternal in our sight. Only the myths which generate our creations are truly eternal.'[5]

Temporary gardens, performance art – we are once again at the garden festival. But Chaumont was the first to impose growth over time as a necessary condition of the work of its participants. It is perhaps more difficult to plan a garden to exist from June to October than one destined to last only a few days, as at most fairs and flower shows. Nonetheless it is this duration, as much as its design-led emphasis, that has inspired imitators elsewhere.

Opposite above Many gardens suggest a quest, even an initiation, leading from one world to another. Thus, visitors moved through the water walls of 'Jardin de passage' (Garden of Passage) by Jean-Pierre Delettre (1997–98).

Right 'Shishi odoshi' refers to watering devices in which the flow of water through bamboo tubes of various sizes can produce random music. These are now common garden ornaments in Japan.

Opposite below In its third year, 'Woven Willows' became a performance piece when the mature lattice-work was regularly enhanced by bursts of rising mist ('Saules dans la brume', 1997).

making time visible

Time is visible through traces left on a place by its past. Landscape architects often regard their terrain as a kind of palimpsest to be read and preserved or incorporated into contemporary design, as the Romantics did with ruins. Home gardeners layer time more intimately, as Hugh Johnson explains: 'A great part of gardening pleasure is the acceptance that one season builds on another. Memory and anticipation are both constantly engaged...'. Seasonal emphasis has existed at Chaumont from its first one-month festival in 1992. That year, the celebrated Danish architect Preben Jakobsen made time visible through his choice of lavish autumn colour.

By 1994, the Festival had reached its current five-month scale. Each year, however, organizers choose to retain a small percentage of the gardens for the following year so that one season can build on another. This has often been due to some solidly built structures worth retaining: the grotto of the Argentinian architect Emilio Ambasz, Fernando Caruncho's pergola, or Hiroshi Teshigahara's bamboo tunnel. Sometimes duration simply meant letting plants grow bigger and thicker, as in the bamboo garden or the woven willow hedging of David and Judy Drew. Less obvious to the public is the artful incorporation of the remains of the previous year into new gardens created by the trainees of the Conservatoire: 'Zingibérales' (1995) was invented to deal with the plant beds left from the 'Potager en l'île' (1994). This recycling has occasionally allowed experiments with growing conditions from season to season, as with the 'Jardin de feuillages géants' (Garden of Giant Leaves, 1994). First imagined as a jungle intended to give children a thrilling experience of exotic scale and texture, it survived the following winter and thus provided useful information about tropical plant growth in a temperate climate.

In 1994 the Atelier Ephémère group produced a spoof of the gardeners' eternal complaint in their installation entitled 'Y-a plus d'saisons' (There Are No More Seasons, 1994). A false snow scene enclosed by tall firs (*Abies nordmanniana*) lay in the centre of a plot brimming with summer-blooming flowers. However, seasonal changes do occur even during the Festival. Visits to Chaumont in early or late summer can give totally different impressions. Bare early on, especially where climbing plants or vegetables are involved, the gardens may delight those who prefer orderly rows and clear prospects. In October, as in any home garden, outlines may be blurred by the exuberance of the vegetation. Despite daily gardening, drought, wind and water damage may have taken their toll but the cornucopia will be at its most abundant. Nothing makes time more visible than a kitchen garden, and these have been numerous at Chaumont since its inception.

Opposite Moving through Hiroshi Teshigahara's bamboo tunnel felt like an initiatory experience. But it was also a giant living sculpture changing yearly until finally overgrown, when it was transformed into a frame for 'Desert Sea'.

Below Using plant growth is one sure way to make time visible. Gardeners experience this daily, but visual artists are now testing the potential more and more often, especially at Chaumont.

Shield ferns (*Dryopteris affinis* and *Polystichum lonchitis*), royal ferns
(*Osmunda regalis*), adder ferns (*Polypodium vulgare*), maidenhair
(*Adiantum venustum)* and ostrich ferns (*Matteucia pensylvanica*)
all helped to soften outlines.

Right Latz observed: 'Fine mist enhancing shapes from time to time
leaves in its wake everything clearer and sharper than before:
colours, air and the quality of light.'

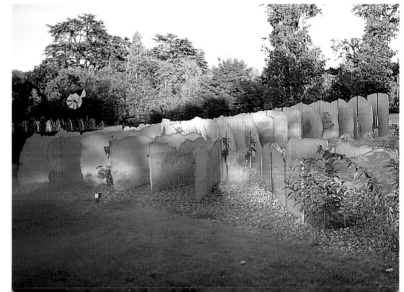

mist garden

nebelgarten 1998–99 Peter Latz, Germany

German landscape architect Peter Latz is famous for many things: his recuperation of industrial sites (such as the people's park at Duisberg-Nord in the Ruhr district), his experiments with alternative technologies and, above all, for landscape architecture incorporating an elegant blending of ecology and minimalism. In an article entitled 'The Idea of Making Time Visible' he explained that

'landscape architecture means capturing the abstract idea of space in elements and layout patterns'.[6] At Chaumont, Latz made time visible in a variety of delightful and mysterious ways, uniting the massive presence of dark stone with the ephemeral, ever-changing qualities of rising mist scintillating in the sun.

'Nebelgarten' was first of all a sequence. Twelve landscape architecture students from Munich helped to place the stone slabs following the lines of a spiral – a shape both metaphorical and narrative which Robert Smithson and George Hargreaves have also

favoured. The spiral design was repeated in details such as the fern fronds, the tendrils of the climbers and the snail shells. High, upright, freestanding stones were placed on the outer edges of the plot, like curtains which both concealed and revealed. In the centre, smaller ones were stacked at an angle, some partially embedded in the ground. Visitors were drawn into the garden by glimpses inwards, the garden's secrets veiled by the constant play of swirling vapours. And as they entered, recounts Latz, 'every position opened new perspectives'.

The motion of water in various forms involved other timescales: 'Fine mist enveloped forms and people from time to time and left everything clearer and sharper than before – colours, air and the quality of light.' Latz compared the movement of the mist to that of a pebble falling into water, making ripples which gradually disappear. But the mist also condensed. It 'ran over the stones, collected itself on the earth in narrow trickles and followed the spiral to its centre…it dropped on leaves, and encouraged mosses to grow on the stones.' For the seasonal growth of plants represented yet another kind of time: low ferns between the blades, wild clematis and aristoloche and moss-covered stones, mint and other water plants at the deepest centre point. The stones themselves incorporated a process of millions of years. Some, brought from Bavaria, contained ammonite fossils, literally brought to light by the play of mist and air around them. 'Change,' wrote Peter Latz, 'was the true sense of this garden.'

Stone slabs – solitary uprights and stacks – were laid out in a spiral pattern. Extracted from a local quarry, they were returned when the garden was dismantled.

Above right 'Time and process lie at the very heart of landscape architecture,' observes the British historian John Dixon Hunt. Latz would surely agree.

nests of the goddess mappa

nids de la déesse mappa 2002 Rémi Duthoit et Eric Barbier, France

Eric Barbier is a sculptor who claims to be both 'at home in the ephemeral' and 'in love with the notion of fertility'. Rémi Duthoit designs gardens which emphasize growth and change. For the eroticism theme, they inherited a plot already dense with semi-wild, 'luxuriant and generous' vegetation around a pond which had sported topiary ducks in 2001. Duthoit is a former student and occasional collaborator of Gilles Clément who encourages gardeners to insert themselves into the existing flux of nature. He was delighted to begin with a piece of land already so lush and alive. Barbier agreed: 'Nature in spring is erotic,' he says, 'young shoots have an energy which is very close to sexual drive.' To complement the existing grasses and reeds, they added large-leaved plants such as gunnera and petasites. Their main aim, however, was to create a seductive nesting site for the goddess Mappa – an invention of Barbier's some years ago – never yet 'found' in a natural habitat.

By the time the Festival opened, several manifestations of the goddess had appeared: bright pink clusters, which only a vulgar mind would recognize as foam-filled latex gloves, suggestive of both teats and hands, offering and inviting caresses. The central one contained a small motor which sent the gloves into a frenzy at unpredictable intervals. And as this was an equal opportunities garden, there were also rows of hanging cucumbers held in bright pink bands (the bottoms of the rubber gloves). Barbier likes sculptures that need tending. He patiently imported cucumbers until the ones planted on site had ripened.

The 'goddesses', carefully displayed in secluded corners, waxed larger as the season progressed. The artists came regularly throughout the season to watch the garden change – and to bring more gloves! Both welcomed surprises, as Duthoit explained: 'I can't make a garden if I know exactly what it will become.' From the start, there was an unexpected chorus of frogs and, later, a leftover rose from the previous year flowered becomingly in pink and white.

Duthoit feels grateful to Clément: 'He taught me to observe my surroundings lovingly, with a kind of joy. To experience gardens as a privileged place for experimentation. To work confidently with whatever is already there.' Clément feels that festival installations deny the intimacy between the gardener and his garden but Mappa's nesting site is an exception. Its whimsy, energy and generosity are clearly those of its creators.

Opposite Sculptor Eric Barbier was delighted to find at Chaumont a site conducive to the nesting of his 'goddess Mappa', a rubber glove creature he imagined years ago. Nesting in several places, she grew as the season progressed.

Designer Rémi Duthoit, influenced by the 'moving garden' explorations of his former teacher, Gilles Clément, happily incorporated grasses and reeds left over from the previous year.

the sound of music

The passage of time in outdoor settings can be artfully organized into sonorous sequences. The landscape historian Alain Corbin recounts that the first contemporary experiments with 'Soundscapes' were the work of the Canadian artist R. Murray Schafer in the 1970s.[7] He points out that sound-defined landscapes offer a completely different mode for perceiving space from their visual counterparts. First of all, they are more transient – sound is rarely durable. They are multidirectional, coming at you from all angles, rather than set in front of the viewer like a panorama. They are usually discontinuous and often mysterious – the person perceiving may not be able to identify what is making the sound. Finally, there is a different quality of penetration: you can close your eyes much more easily than you can block your ears. At the Parc de la Villette in Paris, Bernhard Leitner's *Cylindre Sonore* (Sound Cylinder) whimsically enhances the sunken bamboo gardens of Alexandre Chemetoff intermingled with Daniel Buren's black and white bands.

'Music' in gardens may also mean the random sequences supplied by wind chimes or bird song. The latter implies the presence of living creatures which, like plants, are subject to seasonal variation – birds have their own timetable. At Chaumont, birds regularly nest in welcoming exhibits such as 'Trognes' (1999–2000), a collection of ancient tree trunks. Only two gardens have included birds as part of the design, however, both by the Franco-British team of Edouard François and Duncan Lewis, 'La Fontaine aux oiseaux' (The Bird Fountain, 1997) and 'L'Arbre blanc' (The White Tree, 1996). Organs imitating birdsong are an ancient tradition exploited at Chaumont in 2002 (see p. 116).

The continuous sound of falling water is also considered musical. The effect may be carefully orchestrated to avoid monotonous repetition, as with a dripping tap, and most exhibitors at Chaumont have imagined ways of introducing variations in volume and rhythm. An Italian team from the architecture

Robert Hébrard, a 'musical architect', created 'Lithophonie et pieds dans l'eau' (Lithophone and Feet in Water), a bamboo belfry-waterfall in which the varying flow of water created random musical effects.

and landscape school of Genoa invented 'Goccia a goccia' (Drop by Drop, 1998) which dripped water into small copper dishes or cans. Robert Hébrard, a 'musical architect', created 'Lithophone' (1998) with the Belgian architect Christophe Spehar – a kind of bamboo belfry through which water circulated, triggering a see-saw motion in the bamboo pipes to produce different tones. Adjustments to the amount or speed of water flow varied the results. Hébrard had already used bamboo in 'Shishi odoshi' (1997), designed in collaboration with the Italian designer Daniela Colafranchesci. The title refers to an Asian watering device, another assemblage of bamboo pipes, which filled with water, tilted and spilled over shells and stones. Great numbers of the variously sized assemblages created a continuous series of gentle 'gongs', limited to the plot by a soundproof wall set up against the hedging. Motion and music were further enhanced by the deep red lacquer of pipes set in gravel, surrounded by black and white flowered plants with lanceolate and broad leaves. A striking combination, one might say.

Below and right Architects Duncan Lewis and Edouard François (famous for his Flower Towers) created two installations at Chaumont involving birds, here doves cooing around 'L'Arbre blanc' (The White Tree, 1996).

garden organs

1997–2002 Jean Grelier and Eric Verrier, France, Bartolomeo Formentelli, Italy

Since the 15th century, keyboard instruments have provided music in gardens. Little by little, special water-activated organs were invented for use in parks such as Versailles; one spectacular example has survived at Hellbrunn Palace near Salzburg and two at the Villa d'Este near Rome. Before 2002, Chaumont's most ambitious attempt to continue the tradition was 'L'Orgue hydraulique' (The Water Organ, 1997) of Jean Grelier and Eric Verrier. This postmodern 'garden music box' was meant to reproduce only fragments: the 'noises of nature, of the countryside such as birds, farmyard sounds, bells, and a few snatches of Haydn.' Grelier's mechanism was like a player piano with three rollers set on different time cycles for multiple combinations. The composer Marc Marder suggested incorporating wisps of music arriving as if overheard from a fête at the château beyond, 'phrases through an open window'. Unfortunately, the elaborate structure only worked to plan for one day, but the two water wheels feeding it remained. They have contributed a gentle thud, thud, thud sound, sending water into the canals and pools of neighbouring gardens over many seasons. Several gardens incorporating this structure displayed interesting designs and vegetation, whereas plantings around hydraulic organs generally provide no more than a pleasant floral setting.

In 2002 the water wheels rediscovered their true vocation with 'L'Orgue bucolique' (The Bucolic Organ) of Bartolomeo Formentelli. Since the early 1960s, this legendary craftsman has created or restored 222 organs using only traditional techniques. Born in France of Italian parentage, Formentelli first learned church music with the organ master of Meaux Cathedral. His greatest achievement in France

is his organ restoration at Albi Cathedral. The 'L'Orgue bucolique' specially created for Chaumont, is highly complex: a wooden crank produces the sound of a crow or woodpecker which opens and closes the performances. For the main event, various wind- and water-activated devices imitate panpipes, horns, bells, crickets, warblers, cuckoos and nightingales. For the latter alone, there are five different songs This was after all the year of 'Eroticism in the Garden'.

Sounds can be created singly or in unison to evoke the whole countryside. A sixteen-key, two-octave keyboard also allowed for simple renderings of pieces by Mozart or Haydn. In 2002 different organists came to play (in both senses) all summer long. Usually, however, such a precious instrument could only be opened by official guides, a new note in Chaumont's symphony which usually invited visitor participation. In the winter 'L'Orgue bucolique' migrated indoors to the neighbouring château.

Right above and below Formentelli explains that 'in a great number of very old organs, we used to find, like a little surprise hidden in a garden, sound effects imitating nightingales or cuckoos, activated by a combination of air and water…combined to evoke a forest abounding with hosts of birds.' His instrument at Chaumont is protected in a poplar buffet, which is itself protected by a wicker cage.

'L'Orgue bucolique' was an amazing technical feat which was demonstrated throughout the day by the Chaumont guides during the visits. The surrounding garden here was merely decorative.

storytelling

The carpet bedding displays of 2001 often featured snapshots, frozen moments of developing stories, as here in 'Le Réveil de la tortue' (The Turtle Awakens). Implied narrative can give movement to otherwise static designs.

The word 'narrative' has become a buzzword in garden design today. By definition, narrative sequence involves at least two points in time. As a design category, it may offer 'an alternative to both the abstraction of modernism and the simulations of post-modern culture,' according to Matthew Potteiger and Jamie Purinton. Their categories help to clarify a discourse among critics who may call any allusion to a wider situation a 'story': the history of the garden site and legends, rituals and memorials associated with it, a social problem deliberately evoked by the design and, more generally, various tropes such as metaphor and metonymy, synecdoche and irony, which link the physical presence of the garden to meanings outside its boundaries. One may ask how much explanation visitors should

need in order to grasp specific references, and what forms this information should take. The park at Chaumont is a historic property with its own rich history, but how many of the visitors who appreciated 'India Song' in 1999 knew that its elephant alluded to a gift once made by an Indian prince to the owner of the château? The panels that are posted at the entrance to each garden give some clues, as do the names of the gardens, much like the titles of artworks in general.

Social problems have often been evoked, especially for the 1994 theme 'Imagination During Recession', as in Stefan Tischer's 'Jardin et industrie' (Garden and Industry) depicting the difficulties of the East German economy in an abstract composition of rusted sheet iron, coal and machine debris.

Other designers prefer to keep the story grounded, as it were, so that the garden itself is the story. The two points in time are not, in this case, 'here' and 'beyond', but 'before' and 'after' entry into the garden itself. These gardens mark the age-old mystery of initiation from everyday space into a more mystical world. Jean-Pierre Delettre's 'Jardin de passage' (Garden of Passage, 1997) was one of the most impressive, using semi-transparent water-draped walls to hide a white stone circle diverging, on exit, into two paths, one black and one white. In 2002 'Eroticism in the Garden' produced many variations on the themes of initiation, passage and the labyrinth: 'Le Jardin flou' (Soft and Loose), 'Les Pétales du désir' (The Petals of Desire) and 'Erotica: les chemins de la séduction' (Erotica: The Ways of Seduction) counting among the most explicit.

The controversial *mosaïculture* topic of 2001 was intrinsically anecdotal as shown by such titles as 'Le Réveil de la tortue' (The Turtle Awakens). The proud peacock's story was told by the presence of an egg in the opposite corner of the garden. Some visitors found these designs a little coy, although in some cases narrative added a dynamic element to the otherwise static bedding out.

Garden festivals certainly have their limits. They cannot experiment, as the American architect Kathryn Gustafson points out, with durability and sustainability, so important to many designers today. But temporary gardens that last for only one season can provide a unique context for exploring the performance dimensions of design, whether instantaneous or evolving throughout the season.

Right 'Le Déluge' (1998) by students of the Université de Montréal used garden art to evoke a drama of the outside world: the flooding of the Saguenay region of Quebec in 1996.

Opposite 'Fier comme un paon' juxtaposed a simple white egg to lavishly flaunted colour. Critics dismissed such exhibits as vulgar – as much for their anecdotal quality as for their bedding designs.

from sky to earth

1997–99 Fumiaki Takano, Saido Higuchi, Nobushisa Inuma,
from Takano Landscape Japan; Takano Landscape Taiwan;
Hiroshi Naruse, Naoki Sakan, Naoki Kusumi, Mori from the
Atelier Kaba, Japan

Fumiaki Takano is one of Japan's most highly
regarded landscape architects. The creation by
Takano Landscape Planning at Chaumont told the
following story: 'Water naturally comes down from
the sky, wets the ground creating life, and then
evaporates and returns to the sky…. This is the
eternal cycle.' The team first 'designed a straight line:
water was pumped up by pressure to the top of an
oak tree and then dripped down along a chain.' It
then 'moved and played along the ground, swept
and swirled' into a vortex made of pebbles, Japanese
tiles and light-reflecting glass balls, 'spiralling deeply
into the ground.' Takano considers the spiral to be
'a universal symbol of evolution in nature, and one
of the basic patterns of water.'

On closer inspection, narrative slips out of time
and into symbolism. The cycle represents: 'Birth,
then death, but also reincarnation, which has neither
beginning nor end.' For Takano, this took place
through three spirals collecting water from three
different locations, each with its own level, colour,
shape and place in the story. First and highest was
the 'white place' to the west, with its cloud-decked
pedestal and round forms, then the southern 'red
place' with red pebbles in freer forms and direct
views beyond the garden towards the château.
Deepest and most tranquil was the 'blue place'
with square, horizontal forms and quiet waters.
Takano thus created a union between the French
red, white and blue and the oriental principles of
Fusui with its four legendary creatures placed at
the four cardinal points: a blue dragon, a white tiger,
a red phoenix and a black turtle. Similarly, mingling

Above Takano's ground plan for 'From Sky to Earth' shows a loose
spiral design. It tells the story of moving water while moving itself from
narrative to myth.

Opposite 'In this garden, nothing was left to chance. The
environment outside the plot was taken into account as well as
the château, the trees of the park and the orientation of the terrain'
(Chaumont commentary).

stone from the Loire valley with Japanese plaster pigments reinforced the theme of unity.

Takano was invited to Chaumont by Jean-Paul Pigeat who had admired his Japanese gardens at the Albert Kahn museum near Paris. The Japanese team of eight spent two intense months building at Chaumont, the master even taking his turn with the cooking! Saido Higuchi, the resident head, used techniques of cement design handed down by his father Hiroyasu Higuchi, head of the famous Kaba agency (Team Zoo) which also helped in this creation. Pigeat called this 'an extremely elaborate collective work' and Takano remembers that 'everyone worked with his heart, taking great care.' Chaumont's staff also participated, which lead to 'very joyful exchanges'. The exhibit was so successful that it stayed in place for three years.

Above Loire valley stone intermingled with red, indigo and irridescent plaster pigments brought from Japan by two specialist craftsmen. Like Saido Higuchi's techniques of cement design, their use involved highly skilled traditional lore.

Left Water played with earth here in many ways. Like the spirit of 'joyful exchange' experienced by the team itself, this pleasure was felt by visitors as they moved along the garden paths.

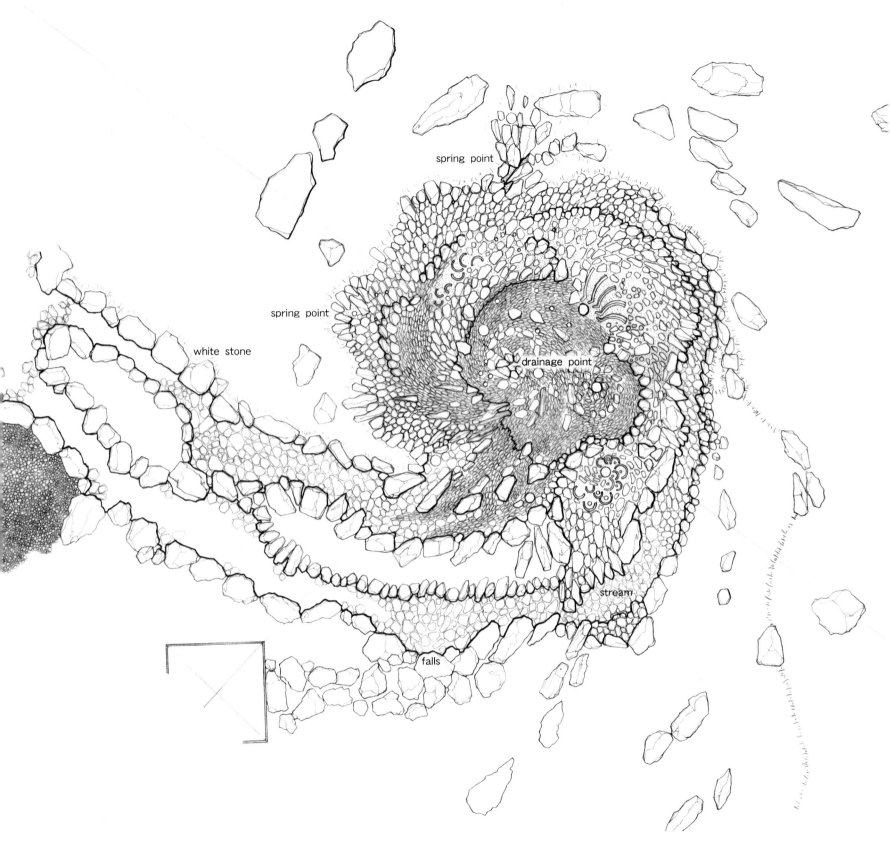

spring point

spring point

white stone

drainage point

stream

falls

Takano writes: 'The spiral is a universal cosmic symbol which is
found everywhere in nature: in the tendrils of morning glory vines, in
the shell of the snail. It suggests the evolution of a force, of a state.'

bricks, bones and pumpkins

jardin des os 2000 Adriaan Geuze, the Netherlands

Adriaan Geuze describes his Chaumont project as a 'still life' made of pot shards, pumpkins and bones. Cow bones, in fact – a deliberate allusion to the outbreak of mad cow disease in Europe in the late 1990s. This installation, a statement about life and death, was intended to make the visitor stop and ask: 'What are we doing with nature?' The bones were for Geuze a challenge to the 'taboo' imposed by the countries that forbade the sale of most meat on the bone at that time. 'You don't expect bones in a garden,' he adds. It was 'totally bizarre'. Geuze also imagined including broken trees, ruins from the destructive storm that battered France in 1999, but this proved too expensive. The terracotta surfacing echoed conventional garden furnishings, but were here broken. In contrast, the pumpkins, 'healthy, fat things', added a note of optimism.

Geuze and his colleagues from West 8, the agency he founded in Rotterdam in 1987, thrive on contrast – the more 'surreal' the better. And this attitude is amply illustrated here: the layout first opposed straight lines and right angles to the unpredictable sprawl of pumpkin growth. The smooth-textured path set off rough shards, soft, scrambling plants and the dry austerity of the bones. Above all, there was the juxtaposition of inert mineral fragments and bones (once alive, now dead) next to exuberant growth. 'Imagine,' Geuze recalls, 'the pumpkins set in gravel, sending out tentacles so that five metres away this large, vital shiny orange thing sits there among the bones'. Seasonal change is part of the picture: 'In late summer the green dies, what remains is a dialogue between death and life.' Green is what one expects in a garden, 'a kind of habit…a cliché of its own.' Here, therefore, green

Adriaan Geuze juxtaposed plant exuberance with formal geometries in a symbolic dialogue between Eros and Thanatos. And since, as he says, 'a garden is always a story', he specifically meant to suggest the tragedy of mad cow disease.

is reduced to a minimum. The accompanying poem at Chaumont read: 'The garden of bones / Orange, white / Life or dead / Entrecôte.'

This was also an artificial landscape – like all of Holland, comments Geuze, asking: 'Is a cow natural?' The West 8 website explains, 'Surreal objects and unexpected twisted realities challenge people to identify and discover'. Not afraid of the word 'soul', West 8 links it to a celebration of 'the heroic and euphoric sentiment of contemporary society and play' to which 'an ironic twist' is given. This is the full euphoria of postmodernism. But for the historian John Dixon Hunt, Adriaan Geuze also 'genuinely refashions our picturesque viewing.'

Plant growth kept an otherwise static composition in motion. Seasonal change became part of the story when the pumpkin vines succumbed to frost during the last days of the Festival in October.

Geuze deliberately kept green to a minimum, toying always with
visitor expectations to impose a provocative and surreal vision.
But like many designers at Chaumont, he used plant growth as
a symbol of optimism.

power plants

1993 Peter Walker, USA

Peter Walker, doyen of American landscape architecture, links his art to American Minimalist painting and to Le Nôtre's French classical design. He also once commented that 'novels are written to express ideas and give people the possibility of discussing these ideas. Why shouldn't a garden

fluorescent tube powered by the panels themselves. 'Flattening' was problematic at Chaumont in a plot with uneven ground, but 'the power of a worked surface' was provided by a field of sunflowers. Their colours were repeated in the two smooth rectangles linking the entrance and heart of the garden. 'The idea,' writes Walker today, 'was to use the sun in different ways, all visible…'. Jane Amidon summarizes the story told by this design: 'A limited palette of paving and planting materials reduced the process of solar energy and photosynthesis into an icon… "Power Plants" explored various manifestations of the nature-technology dialectic under the guise of sunbathing, the cultivation of an agricultural crop and the collection and dispersal of solar energy.' But at the same time, this design was autonomous.

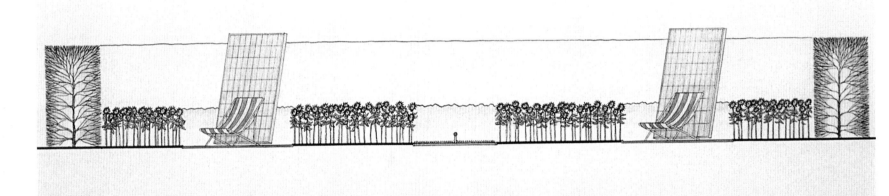

Sunflowers, deckchairs and solar panels all paid homage to the source of power that inspired this witty design while creating interlocking visual patterns.

be designed for exactly the same purpose?' Questions of form do not preclude social issues: 'Minimalism in landscape architecture…suggests an artistically successful approach to dealing with two of the most critical environmental problems we currently face: mounting waste and dwindling resources.' Walker rejects postmodern fragmentation in favour of 'reduction and focus…mystery rather than irony'.

'Power Plants', Walker's garden at Chaumont, illustrated the landscape architect's tenets while maintaining sensuous appeal in its own right.[8] 'Seriality' and the typically modernist grid were lightly evoked by the symmetrical spacing of eight solar panels, each fronted by a striped deckchair with a contrasting blue-and-white pattern. 'Gesture' was present as a strong central axis and a green

In Walker's phrase, it was: 'held by the organization of the objects within' – like minimalist painting.

And what of time and change? Walker's large-scale urban works often give an impression of immutability. Here, causality was playfully illustrated: the sun shone, the panels absorbed and the green light glowed. The sunflowers grew and turned their heads to the sun. Walker's writing on this subject recalls Wallace Stevens's jar mentioned in Chapter 3: 'Minimalism has to do with light, weather and the seasons and how they can be read against an artefact. This artefact can be something very simple… it took me years to get just this little bit of information clear in my mind.'

Above Walker's formal geometries adapted to the shape of the Chaumont plot but uneven ground was problematic. The sea of sunflowers helped to regularize it, creating 'surface' and 'seriality'.

Left Walker's 'gesture' here was the thermometer which cleverly emphasized the central axis. Its temperature rose as the panels absorbed sunlight. The cycle of energy kept moving.

5

the landscape
question

Festival gardens are sometimes dismissed as rootless installations in cookie-cutter spaces. Some of their temporary creations are site-related, even site-determined, but most are transferable if not actually transportable. For that very reason, however, they raise important issues about 'spirit of place'. One of these is the controversial link between 'garden' and 'landscape'.

Many consider, like Roberto Burle Marx, that gardens simply provide 'a transition between architecture and landscape.' More specifically, the historian John Dixon Hunt posits first uncultivated nature, second agricultural nature and third ornamental nature, as in gardens. Still others, such as the French philosopher Augustin Berque, see landscape not as a physical reality but as an attitude, a projection of the human mind. Ancient China and the West today are 'landscape cultures' but many are not.

One can consider landscape without gardens, but not gardens without landscape. A garden always bears some relationship to its setting: it may define itself against the outside world, be a concentration of it or an imitation so artful that the two blend seamlessly together. Rejection, reflection, allusion, inclusion – all these relationships with the surrounding landscape may appear singly or together in a garden. It is precisely this kind of complexity that leads Dixon Hunt to conclude that 'the most sophisticated form of landscape architecture is garden art'. He compares landscape and garden respectively to prose and poetry. He claims that landscape, like prose, can be everything from a shopping list to a great novel, but poetry always has pretensions to art.

By some ironic quirk of fate, however, it is the prose of landscape architecture rather than the poetry of garden design that has retained the higher standing in Western culture. For decades architects have scorned designers as ignorant and unprofessional promoters of bucolic escapism, as far removed from art as candyfloss. Landscape architecture requires more rigorous formal training, has stronger intellectual and academic connections and is more often practised by men engaged in prestigious careers. Garden design often attracts older women trying to make a living, whose work can be too easily dismissed as emotional and decorative. Still further below on the conventional ladder are the hands-on gardeners, as intellectual abstraction is more esteemed than manual labour, however creative.

Garden festivals – Chaumont in particular – challenge these dreary hierarchies. The approach established over the years dissolved the distinction between designers, architects and hands-on gardeners, with women involved in all activities as much as men. Many participants hire contractors to realize their designs, but many also come to dig and build with their own hands. The general approach is that of the designers Eric Ossart and Arnaud Maurières who insist that 'landscaping is not a profession but a condition; anyone who gardens, lays out a road, even draws in the sand, is imagining a landscape.' Dixon Hunt concurs when he defines all related activities as 'exterior place-making'.

A garden festival is a good place to explore the lyric poetry of such exterior place-making in concentrated form. After all, if Jean-Paul Pigeat called his event a landscape festival, far fewer people would visit it.

Opposite above Bernard Wolgensinger's 'Désert noir auvergnat' (Black Auvergne Desert, 1994) condensed the Auvergne's volcanic landscape into a series of symbols.

Right For the 'Vallon des brumes', the Chaumont team arranged a piece of their home landscape, the ravine separating the château park from the Festival grounds.

Opposite below The rice paddies created by Arnaud Maurières and his students (1997) were both a direct quotation from a foreign landscape and a symbolic stylization.

games with scale

Many festival gardens concentrate specifically on landscape as both their theme and inspiration. Landscapes can be 'represented' in many ways. The simplest is direct quotation, where the scale remains the same but only a fragment of the larger scene is transposed – as when the architect Kisho Kurokawa planted a sample of tropical rain forest in the very heart of the new airport of Kuala Lumpur.[1] At Chaumont, 'La Rizière' (1997) displayed a piece of rice paddy with its undulating contours, while the Palestinian wall borrowed a small section of terracing from Bethlehem. When the model is a garden rather than a larger landscape, it is easier to imitate without changing the scale. Lynden B. Miller's 'New England Garden' could very well be imagined in a similarly sized plot in Connecticut or Vermont. On the other hand, Rachid Koraïchi's Algerian courtyard might actually be smaller on a home site.

More often, in a typical Chaumont plot measuring 2,690 square feet (250 square metres) reference to a model outside means representation on a reduced scale. The tradition is ancient: historians claim that the hanging gardens of Babylon were a stylized re-creation of distant mountains, and garden fountains were an image of mountain springs.[2] Jean Mus, a leading Riviera designer, condensed a Mediterranean landscape and garden by mixing plants typical of the wild *garrigue* and southern gardens: olive trees, myrtle, rosemary, cistus and bougainvillea in 'La Côte d'Azur' (The Côte d'Azur, 1994). But scale can also be enlarged and magnified. Serge Mansau's 'Réflexion dans une flaque d'eau' (Puddle Reflection, 2001) created giant willow leaves which dwarfed viewers (see p. 180). The Chaumont home team was among the first to use large-leafed, architectural foliage to create a delicious sense of disorientation in small spaces. These games were often planned for children, as in 'Barbibulle' (Barbibubble, 1997) or the miniature jungles made for the Société Pro Urba.

'Barbibulle' (Barbibubble, 1997) used giant pebbles and foliage so that visitors felt like tiny creatures moving in the vegetation. This sort of game was often aimed at children.

Above Games created by the Société Pro Urba involved water devices and sprinkler systems. Part of the playfulness was a miniature jungle of large-scale plants for children to get lost in.

Left 'Potager en l'île' (Island Potager, 1994) provided more water fun among giant exotics including the hardy banana tree (*Musa basoo*).

living walls

murs végétaux 1994–97 Patrick Blanc, Michel Mangematin, France

Patrick Blanc's 'Murs végétaux' astonished the public at Chaumont during the four years they were exhibited and have now been re-created as part of the Conservatoire's permanent gardens. Initially, the architect Michel Mangematin laid out three slightly curved walls each facing in a different direction, including one rising from a small pool. Blanc overlaid the metal and plastic structures with a fabric of his own invention and planted several hundred different plants in its pockets. His choices were definitely 'site-determined' – their orientation and even distance from the ground created very specific microclimates. Since then, he has planted similar walls in places as varied as the Fondation Cartier in Paris, Renzo Piano's Aquarium building in Genoa and the Vivendi experimental water gardens at Méry-sur-Oise near Paris. No two walls are alike; each is minutely adjusted to local climate and growing conditions. 'You will never find my walls in kit form,' he jokes. Imitators lack both his vast plant expertise and his sharp eye.

Blanc views his hanging gardens not merely as scientific experiments with varied microclimates but as miniature landscapes. He describes the 85-foot-high (26-metre) wall he created for a hotel courtyard in Paris as 'a forest atmosphere to make people dream', an 'entire landscape, not a garden, not just a tapestry or a painting.' A specialist in how plants adapt to their environment, Blanc views any urban jungle as one biotope among many – one he adores just as he loves wilderness. He is not so sure about gardens: 'A garden takes people's time and room. But imagine coming out of the underground face to face with a hanging jungle fragment, right there, like a gift!'

Only a knowledgeable botanist can chose plants for each microclimate: top or bottom, back or front. Larger shrubs at the top create a canopy effect.

Above and left In the first year, the 'Murs végétaux' were planted with a dense mix which included *Artemisia ludoviciana*, bergenias, box, hostas, creeping plants like campanulas, *Geranium macrorrhizum album* 'Spessart', lamiums, saxifrages, oreganos and corydalis, upright-growing fennel, sedem spectabile and ligularia, grasses including *Elymus glaucus*, strange exotics like *Beschorneria yuccoides* and large shrubs such as *Cotinus coggygria* 'Royal Purple'.

It took him ten years to develop successful hydroponic techniques, which he has now copyrighted. By 1985, he had found the ideal planting medium which he calls 'aquaturf': a blend of peat and synthetics which can retain water and liquid fertilizers and form pockets for plants. Blanc claims that his vertical gardens require ten times less water and feeding than the same plants in the ground. They can also be much more densely planted. The rich intermingling at Chaumont evolved over the years to include collections of fuchsias, and in 1997, a small cataract. Nature added its own contributions, self-sown buddleias for example. Blanc's intricate plant associations are as astonishing as his technical mastery. The result is strikingly beautiful.

Above Quickly filled in, these lush miniature landscapes often welcome unexpected visitors such as buddleias, as in any natural biotope.

Left Patrick Blanc has created vertical gardens all over France and Europe. No two walls are ever the same, and they evolve constantly.

Michel Mangematin's layout permitted many microclimates: wet or dry, in the sun or shade at different times of day and facing in different directions.

the pampas:
from monotony to infinity

pampa, vers l'infini par la monotonie Martina Barzi and
Josefina Casares 2001–2002, Argentina

Martina Barzi and Josefina Casares speak for
themselves: 'A guiding rule in our professional work
has been to always look for a simple idea that
epitomizes the spirit to be transmitted by each
particular design. We have been in quest of a
national style –as opposed to the "copies" that our
clients propose after their trips abroad – and, now
that we are principals of the John Brookes School
of Garden Design in our country, we aim to shape
truly Argentine landscape designers. PAMPA INFINITA
is the name chosen for our new school of design
arts…. To us, this project is intermingled with
motherhood, love for our land, the excitement and
responsibility of teaching and, above all, the pure
joy of the creative act.

The Pampa, land of cows, says everything it
has to say in a square meter, but repeats it in the
millions of kilometres that make up the greater part
of Argentina. As Victoria Ocampo puts it so well:
"America, where the dimension, multiplication and
monotony are so evident, colours our soul…our
Pampa, our river, stretch to the infinite by the
horizontal line."

The Argentinian perception of space is
expressed through subtle undulating shapes,
chromatic monotone and constant repetition. Plants
are not treated as individual specimens, since the
Pampa never shows the whimsical detail and varied
combination found in an English meadow, but only
great areas of different tints: earth, wheat, sun-
scorched grass, the baked mud besides dried river
beds and dew ponds. In the Chaumont presentation,
the deck hovers over "nature", the only man-made

element in a sea of grass. The dry river beds are
represented by white stone, while raw hide brings
into the design yet another intrinsic feature of the
Pampa: cattle. Stubble is simulated by swan pipes
or rods which stand out against the black soil. The
wind blowing through this stubble of golden pipes
plays the sound of unlimited space.

The sun-scorched colour of stipas (feather grass)
cover yet another area; and an endless repetition of
the design is contrived by mirrors placed at intervals
along the hedge. "The plains of Patagonia are

boundless…they bear the stamp of having lasted
as they are now, for ages, and there appears to be
no limit to their duration through future time." (Charles
Darwin, *The voyage of the Beagle*).'

Above Some admirers of 'Pampa' compared its conception of
space and use of mirrors to the mazes and time factor in the works
of Argentinian writer Jorge Luis Borges.

Above and left A vast landscape of earth, wheat, sun-scorched grass and stubble is condensed and abstracted. White-stone curves represent dried river beds. The mirrors provide vertical contrast, help to cut off this world from the outside, enrich the abstract assemblage of coloured fragments and open this small space to infinity.

symbolic landscapes

Any condensation of landscape easily slips into symbols, abstraction, even minimalism: Bernard Wolgensinger's stunning 'Désert noir auvergnat' (Black Auvergne Desert, 1994) thus reduced the hills and ravines of a volcanic Auvergne landscape into a display of black basalt with white marbles representing quartz crystals. 'Trognes' (1999) used synecdoche, the part for the whole, in a more rustic presentation: massive tree trunks salvaged from hedges pulled up in western France evoked an extensive rural tradition of pollarding. Chinese and Japanese gardens have made symbolic landscape miniaturization a main focus of their art to the present day. At Chaumont in 1993, Shodo Suzuki created 'L'Archipel (The Archipelago) as a model Zen garden, but included broken pieces of rock representing the fragmentation of contemporary Japanese society. Suzuki, a 'living national treasure' in Japan, donated this garden to Chaumont on condition that it remain there until his death, incorporating a 'borrowed' view of the river and château beyond.

Certainly, the reduction of landscape to symbol is one of any festival's most common approaches. So much so that many of Chaumont's best examples have already been cited in other chapters. The meadows evoked in Chapter 2 seem at first glance a mere borrowing of landscape fragments, but they often have symbolic subtexts. In 'Sillon romand' (1996) the meadow's double furrows displayed city uniformity on one side and country variety on the other. Some of the best 'contrary gardens' (see Chapter 6) adopt condensed and symbolic landscape as a way of challenging our assumptions about life and death.

This tendency may also lead to purely abstract compositions where allusions, though rich, no longer involve any reference to a physical setting beyond: 'Mente la menta?' and 'Code naturel' have become dream landscapes of their own, visions apart.

Opposite Shodo Suzuki's 'L'Archipel' (The Archipelago) used broken fragments of polished stone to symbolize a crisis in Japanese culture. The circle suggested the Satori of a Buddhist monk. The nearby Loire river evoked the passage of life.

Below and right The writer Alexandre Vialatte's text *L'Auvergne absolu* inspired Bernard Wolgensinger's 'Désert noir auvergnat' (Black Auvergne Desert): 'The Auvergne is a childhood memory. A black memory…black abbeys, the black stone of Volvic…'. A 'desert' of grasses and basalt contrasted with inverted cones and hanging plants inside the tent-volcano.

the earth in motion

la terre en marche 1996 George Hargreaves, USA

George Hargreaves currently chairs the Department of Landscape Architecture at the Harvard University Graduate School of Design. Committed mainly to large-scale public projects, he rejects the common oppositions between ecology and industry, nature and culture, insisting rather that 'most landscapes have such complex histories they can never again be "natural".'[3] His sculpted land forms 'foster an awareness' of dynamic natural process by manipulating local 'light, shadow, water, wind; residual environmental and industrial remnants; topography and habitat'. Most are therefore 'site-generated'. Yet Hargreaves does not reject 'event spaces' and performance aspects in landscape architecture. His creation for Chaumont beautifully summarizes his approach in capsule, ephemeral form. The lecture he gave the same year at the Rencontres de Chaumont was called '(Re)made Landscapes'.

The Loire river inspired 'La Terre en marche'. Visible from the conical hill that dominates the design, it was also echoed in the serpentine land forms which 'allude to riverine processes and hydrodynamics, but are transformed through technological means into

earthen rather than fluid matter.' Hargreaves's own summary provides a clear picture: 'A square gravel plinth provides a level surface for orientation upon entry. A grove of fiberglass poles that quiver either in the wind or upon human disturbance forms an entry to the plinth and addresses the question central to the festival: "Is Technology Poetically Correct?" Combined with a trembling perforated steel bench set off against a bed of equisetum grass, the grove forms a poetic bridge between technology and ecology, yet admits their disunion. The disparity between the tightly mown grass on the surface of the conical hill and the high grass left to grow untamed on the serpentine landforms similarly underscores both the connections and the distinctions between natural and technological. A mix of white perennials forms a mat on the leftover side of the serpentines to provide varied sculptural contrasts rendered in vegetation.'

Many aspects of this design recall Hargreaves's famous Villa Zapu landscape in California's Napa Valley: sculpted land forms representing natural processes with an ecological message; carpets of contrasting plants creating undulating geometries;

Hargreaves's hill allowed views of the Loire river, inspiring in its 'riverine processes and hydrodynamics'. His symbolism was both site-specific and universal.

focus on a single, high viewpoint and allusions to the site's specific characteristics, here the Loire. Hargreaves's work has variously been classified as 'picturesque' because of his emphasis on process, 'classic' because of his return to strong, simple, even archetypal forms like the spiral, and a postmodern adaptation of land art to landscape practice.[4] Whatever the label, this garden gracefully condenses elemental process into a small festival plot.

Formal patterns could be appreciated as elegant detailing on ground level, but only an aerial view revealed the spiral in its minimalist entirety. Like many land art creations, this garden was aided by aerial photography.

rhapsody in blue

rapsodie en bleu 1995 Jacques Simon, France

Artificial beech trees with metallic leaves caught the Loire valley light and tinkled seductively in the wind. But they symbolized man's destruction of nature.

Jacques Simon has been a legend in France for fifty years. He was a pioneer in devising people-friendly landscaping for cheap housing developments, and his Saint-John-Perse park in Reims has become a pilgrimage site for professional designers. He was the first in France to experiment with land art: his field-size European flag made with bachelor's buttons and calendula lives on in many memories – and in many books.[5] He has claimed that the only two important viewpoints for a landscape architect are from a tractor and from the air. Gardens, 'calculated arrangements where plants reign', are not of great interest to him; his affinities are with working-class suburbs and small farms. But he has almost a cult for trees – beech, hornbeam, birch – which, grouped and planted on artfully graded hillsides, can provide serenity and a kind of community salvation.

Writer, publisher and teacher, Simon was influenced by American thinkers like Henri David Thoreau and Ian McHarg, who invited him to teach in Philadelphia in 1960. Thirty years later, he was the first to win the *Grand prix du paysage* bestowed by the French government. In recent years he has been preoccupied with ecological issues and the endangered French countryside.

At Chaumont in 1995 Simon produced a symbolic space evoking the state of landscape in general. A huge dead tree trunk, sectioned and piled up, contrasted with a grove of metal monkey-puzzle trees and artificial beeches glittering with silvery-blue foliage. Stone, concrete and polished blue glass on the ground formed patterns around a central enclosure of wood and reflective steel. Inside could be glimpsed a blue figure emerging from the ground: the Gardener. His goggled gaze was fixed on a single tuft of thick, luxuriant grass.

The accompanying commentary refers to the destruction of nature and the reappearance of life and hope. Simon's own notes describe the scene as both 'a macabre farce', and 'a subversion and ecstasy suspended between fiction and reality'. It is 'a filter, both place and non-place.... The character emerging from the earth is the self-portrait of each of us, apparently petrified between pleasure and guilt.... The outlines on the ground are a kind of artificial fairyland, the trees are messengers from a world before language, the metallic enclosure is like a cradle...'. Above all, 'the garden invites the visitor to metaphysical reflections about the world.'

Above and left Artificial monkey-puzzle trees rose against a
background of stone, concrete and blue glass. In the secret heart
of the garden, the Gardener emerges from the earth, mesmerized
by the only green and growing presence in this design. Once more,
plant growth symbolizes hope in an abstract, artificial setting.

context

'Spirit of place' is not entirely absent from garden festivals. Each of the new events has its own environment. In Canada and Sweden, exhibition plots are like clearings in a wilderness to which they allude, while in Lausanne and Berlin temporary garden festivals fill bustling city centres. At Chaumont the gardens occupy part of the unfinished 19th-century park by Achille Duchêne, extending out from an experimental farm, itself attached to a Renaissance château. The latter's towers are clearly visible from many of the gardens and 'borrowed' for their designs. It is in some ways an ideal festival terrain, where Dixon

The Festival ground, measuring over three hectares, is laid out on the plateau, bordered on one side by the new housing developments and on the other, by a deep ravine. This serves as a kind of moat separating the Festival from both the farm buildings and the historic park. To enter its enclosure from the latter side, you must pass through a mock-wood turret and bridge, both dating from the early 20th century. Their fairy-tale aspect is quite in the spirit of contemporary Chaumont. The bridge overlooks the 'Vallon des brumes' (Misty Vale) below, one of the site's permanent gardens.

The hornbeam hedges that surround Festival plots and have a single point of entry might seem to cut them off from the world outside, while imposing the traditional English arrangement of banked colour against a green curtain with a single, privileged viewpoint. Rarely has this happened, however. Most gardens obey the conditions recommended by Peter Walker in his essay on 'Gardens without Walls': they 'do not depend on being bordered even though they may have borders' but 'are held by the organization of the objects within'. Nor have the boundaries – necessary in the setting – proven an insurmountable obstacle to designers wanting to make use of the physical surroundings or context. Many play with the boundary lines by spilling outside of them. Thus one garden made an incisive statement about the sprawling suburbia beyond the walls of the Chaumont Conservatoire. In 'Lointain extérieur' (View Beyond, 1993) an observation platform rising from a sea of white nicotiana let visitors look through binoculars at a countryside threatened by anarchic construction.

Anyone working at Chaumont soon discovers the subtly changing light of the Loire valley. Architects from the nearby city of Tours, very familiar with these conditions, chose as their theme the Loire river, visible from the park, for 'Mouvements de Loire' (The Flowing Loire, 2001). Motivated by the recent classification of the region by UNESCO as a World Heritage Site, they took inspiration from the willows that grow along the river banks. In their presentation they quoted the writer Julien Gracq, describing the local landscape: 'Willow leaves, with their lanceolate

Designers from the city of Tours took inspiration from the Loire river and the willow trees along its banks. Many artists have referred to the Loire in their gardens at Chaumont, often including glimpses of the river in their designs.

Hunt's three 'natures' – woodland, farmed fields and gardens – all converge. At the same time the historic past (the château park) and the present (suburban communities outside the gates) surround each year's collection of future-oriented gardens.

elegance and silky, silver undersides, have a texture that adds to the Loire's special quality of light, makes the wind's transparency visible, takes part in the fluidity, the undulation, the shimmering aspects of the river, a genuine choreography with the contours of the islands.' Willow-leaf patterns are repeated in several materials of this installation, the most striking example being the flowing stainless-steel cut-outs serving as walls.

The spaces surrounding individual hedged plots at the Festival offer another kind of context. Planted originally by Eric Ossart and the Chaumont

create a kind of meadow environment, an idealized countryside. At the bottom of the hill lie Chaumont's 'wild' gardens, one of which is the 'Vallon des brumes', where a meandering stream lends itself to artificial misting devices and to a plant palate enriched by the botanist Patrick Blanc following an expedition to Japan. 'Wild' here (as elsewhere) covers plantings that are seemingly free-form, though deliberately and outrageously artificial. The aim is to enhance the natural disposition of the site by the designers' intervention. The walk through the valley floor is magical.

gardeners (as of 1996), they echo both first and second nature, untamed and cultivated land. Ossart's experiments mixing tall grasses and roses, later used for the Roseraies at Blois and Orléans and 'Le Jardin de l'alchimiste' (The Alchemist's Garden) in Provence,

'Spirit of place' at Chaumont is thus adapted to the spirit of the Festival itself. Whether in the plots themselves or in the surrounding spaces, the emphasis is placed on diversity treated with imagination and wit.

Left and above The 'Vallon des brumes' is Chaumont's 'wild' garden linking the château park and the Festival grounds. Visitors can meander along it before climbing up either side, or they can cross directly over it on the whimsical mock concrete bridge made c.1900.

'Le Triangle d'eau', far from being a foreign object imposed on a Chaumont clearing, was like a delicate sensor capturing it. The electric prism was carefully positioned in proximity to the existing tree trunk.

Right Tahara specifically plans contrasts in scale: outside nature enters through reflections in the moving water, but also finds an echo in the tiny island of moss and stone.

Opposite Tahara's mastery of motion, reflection, inversion and chiaroscuro have caused his work to be described as baroque. Here the natural landscape of Chaumont moves constantly across his triangle.

the water triangle

le triangle d'eau 1998 Keiichi Tahara, Japan

Keiichi Tahara practises an art he calls 'light sculpture photography'. This means many things – projections and 'light installations' such as the rainbow ribbons illuminating the vaults over the Canal Saint Martin in Paris; solid objects like stone slabs which seem to absorb photographic fragments of baroque art; vast landscape scenes including the pillars of light, 'crystal totems', leading into the ocean at the Mont Saint

Michel in Normandy. Even gardens, like the black-and-white gravel Niwa Garden of the Maison européenne de la photo in Paris. All of his works draw into themselves the world around them. Its substance is absorbed by the very materials used, and its reflections, through light.

The water triangle at Chaumont was a flat black slab slightly tilted towards the plot's entrance, its apex set close to the trunks of two beech trees, pointing at mixed greenery of varied height and volume. The strong dark hedge line of Chaumont's plots was visible only on the sides. Water flowed continuously over the triangle, reflecting the mixed foliage canopy, the sky and passing clouds. It rippled gently as it emerged from a central fountain before being recycled. Two vertical accents added complexity: first a tall electric prism rising parallel to the nearby tree trunks, which turned white or golden when lit; secondly, a framed woman's torso, photographed with such striking shadow effects that each body part seemed to float separately – a hand, a breast. This stunning chiaroscuro echoed the contrast between the dark triangle and the white pillar. As Keiichi Tahara explained in an interview in 1999, 'white light represents sensations, impressions, emotions, while black is the interiority of the creative imagination'.[6]

Art critics compare Tahara's work to the European baroque, especially in their melding of opposites such as sky and water. In 'Le Triangle d'eau', a small island of moss and pebbles echoed the leafy frame outside, with such a contrast of scale that perception fell into a gap between inseparable opposites. His inspiration was both Japanese and European. As a child he swam in ponds near Kyoto, already captivated by reflections among natural elements, including the trunks of pine trees. When Tahara first came to France in 1972, he found Parisian light harsh compared with that of Kyoto. The idea for the garden came after a long walk by the Loire river and it is perhaps in the Loire valley that he recovered something of the humid and ever-changing luminosity of his own Japan.

wild iron path

sentier de fers sauvages 1998+ (a permanent garden)
Jean Lautrey plus the Conservatoire international des parcs
et jardins et du paysage, France

In the wild ravine bordering the Festival ground,
sculptor Jean Lautrey imagined a series of garden
follies melting into the natural setting – highly romantic
false 'ruins' half-smothered in vegetation. Lautrey
took inspiration from a poem by Rainer Maria Rilke
which, much like Paul Verlaine's famous *Fêtes
galantes*, evokes abandoned château gardens:
'They dress in light shades when spring reappears
and burn with a slow flame in autumn through
branches intertwined, like arabesques made from
the wrought iron of the gates…'.[7] When Lautrey
built the follies (which he did himself with his son
Gaspard), they worked 'totally immersed' in the
sound of Vivaldi's sonata no. 12, 'La Folia', first
clearing a trail through the ocean of brambles.

The *fers sauvages* are the steel reinforcing rods
used in building construction, and which are here
deliberately allowed to rust. Visitors first encounter
them surrounding a woodland amphitheatre made
of tree trunks fashioned into seats. People often
picnic here and there are occasional performances
by actors or musicians, sheltered by overhanging
ash branches. Follows a series that is both playful
and beautiful, to be experienced and not merely
admired: a curving tunnel made of arched iron rods;
a miniature iron suspension bridge over the half-
collapsed ravine, hung with mosses, an uncertain
ghost of faraway city cousins; a giant tree trunk made
of soldered metal around three existing trees, which –
thanks to the change of scale – look like new shoots.
The metal stump supports a flat section of sequoia
used as a terrace, just large enough for lovers, which
gives onto a splendid view of the château. Below,
a cavern suggests some mysterious inhabitant.

Lautrey's mock ruins transform a wild Chaumont lanscape into art,
recalling the romantic tradition of picturesque decay which produced
so many garden follies.

Left and above Richard Weller's judgement fits Lautrey's work well: 'Rather than speak of landscape, which is an 17th–18th-century term, it seems more appropriate today to speak of "fabric" or "field". Fabrics are mixtures of materials; often what we once categorised as a mixture of the natural and the unnatural.'

Last in the series is an iron gate under an old horse-chestnut tree, half-buried in honeysuckle, a rambling rose and more blackberry shoots, built at a strange angle as if half-fallen.

Lautrey often works as a scenographer. The 'Sentier de fers sauvages' certainly transforms untamed landscape into artful 'representation' in the manner of Wallace Stevens's jar upon the hill in Tennessee (see p. 76), or of traditional garden follies. But Lautrey's sculptures also echo the picturesque tradition which blurs the distinction between representation and landscape.[8] Seemingly born from the site itself, they successfully maintain this difficult balance, discreet as spider webs but never invisible.

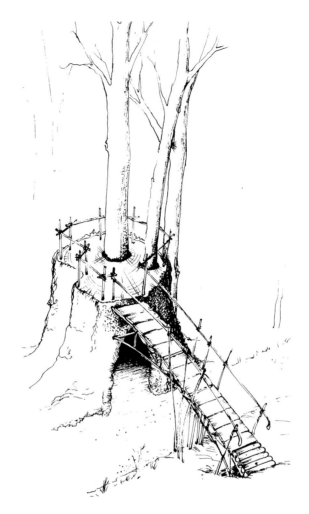

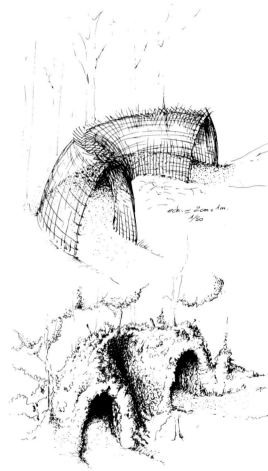

Above The sculptor's mock stump makes living trees look like shoots that reappeared after cutting, but on a giant scale. The tiny terrace offered views of the château opposite.

Right Lautrey's drawings show the tunnel as constructed with builders' reinforcing rods, then at a later stage covered with vegetation so that it melted into the setting.

Opposite Like spider webs in a garden, these sculptures can be discovered only by looking twice. They reward close inspection but also enhance surrounding perspectives and changing light.

wit and whimsy

Gardens are often experienced as pastoral visions, havens of idealized nature, refuges like the Forest of Arden or the gardens of Bocaccio which kept tyrants and plagues at bay. Does humour belong in the garden or with the hostile forces outside? Historians generally view jokes such as Renaissance water jets as exceptions if not aberrations.[1] Yet humour, irony, and pastiche are found today in the design repertoire, especially at Chaumont.

The French poet Baudelaire wrote an essay on laughter in which he imagined Virginie, a pure young heroine, arriving in Paris. Full of angelic and sentimental idealism, Virginie sees a caricature in a shop window – a nasty, salacious and mean-spirited piece of satire. Far from laughing, she is repulsed. But the longer she lives in the city, the more inclined she is to laugh. Baudelaire suggests that laughter is corrupt, diabolical and incompatible with innocence.

There are gardens like Virginie and designers who mock them, objecting, like the American landscape architect Ian McHarg, to any 'reassurance that nature is benign, bountiful, sentimental, and peaceful'. McHarg flatly denies 'that God is more accessible from a garden',[2] while Ian Hamilton Finlay placed an armoured tank in his 'Et in Arcadio ego'. Bucolic gardens, claim their critics, thrive on cliché and conformity, the enemies of art. One faction in French landscape architecture still condemns private gardens as vectors of sentimental bourgeois escapism and blames the Festival for encouraging them! But Chaumont is on the side of laughter…

It was postmodernism that first introduced an aesthetic of pastiche and parody, embracing street culture as well as the avant-garde, exulting in fragmented, free-floating images.[3] As John Dixon Hunt expressed it: 'Some contemporary place makers invoke representational strategies almost satirically, as if to avail themselves of their scope while distancing themselves from potential banalities (Martha Schwartz's bagel garden or the gilded frogs in Atlanta).' Banality, like the bagel, can become the very stuff of art – if taken with tongue in cheek. Garden gnomes appeal to Baudelaire's heirs who find in kitsch a whacky world of inspiration precisely because it is the opposite of middle-class good taste. Chaumont has from its first year challenged prevailing convention by encouraging such vulgarities as the recycled materials common in working-class allotments. Annual themes have included carpet bedding, eroticism and in 2003, weeds.

Postmodernism celebrated the 'carnavalesque' as described by the Russian historian Mikael Bahktine, an inversion of conventional logic and values which could be satirical and aggressive to the point of revolution, but also delight in play for its own sake. Baudelaire also praised the 'absolute comic' where wit moves beyond satire to pure poetry, evocative of childhood fancies. Chaumont offers all these variants. Many view the Festival as heir to the 1968 movement in Paris when students demanded the right to 'take their dreams for reality'.

The Chaumont team takes care, however, to invite representatives of all factions – even Virginie's. Charles Dard, professor at the conservative Ecole nationale supérieure du paysage at Versailles, comments 'Not only is Pigeat not a snob, he is not racist. He even invites architects. It's a tradition with him!'[4] Humour works for tolerance here, whether satire, irony or parody, pure nonsense or poetic delight.

Opposite above Many visitors deemed the mouldering mobile home of 'La Fuite' (Leaky Escape, 1997) to be the epitome of bad taste. Its creator Macha Makeieff is famous for satirical theatre productions.

Right Chaumont's 'Baobab', a fantastical tree that combines eternal tears with everlasting bloom, became a symbol of the Festival spirit – witty, multi-cultural and artificial though rooted in the natural world.

Opposite below 'Trois cabanes' (Three Huts) had garden shelters for the Three Little Pigs, a whimsical childhood fancy elaborated for pure pleasure in the spirit of Baudelaire's *comique absolu*.

contrary gardens

Frédérique Garnier's 'Le Jardin hostile' (The Hostile Garden, 1995) used only prickly plants such as *Echinops ritro* 'Veitch Blue' and eryngiums, including *E. agavifolium*, *E. alpinum* 'Blue Star' and *E. planum*.

Opposite above Gardens are rooted, but the fold-up kitchen garden in 'Potager nomade' (Nomadic Kitchen Garden, 1999) challenges our most basic assumptions.

Opposite The title 'Le Jardin hostile' punned on the French *le jardin ose-t'il?* (does the garden dare?). At Chaumont it does.

In Marcel Pagnol's novel *Jean de Florette*, the villain exults: 'I plug the springs, I plant brambles, I graft dog roses, I am the devil's peasant!'[5] Contrary gardens may mock conventional expectations by simply reversing some familiar usage, drawing our attention to cliché in a witty manner. The carnival world beloved of postmodern practitioners is always topsy-turvy and inside out. Massachusetts designer Michael Blier won an American Landscape Architecture Association award for a creation at Chaumont where he grew trees upside down and provided trampolines so visitors could jump up to the roots (1998). Swiss designers Gérald and Geneviève Poussin created a miniature golf course called 'Centre d'accueil pour les nuisibles' (Welcome Centre for Pests, 1993). Obstacles took the form of painted metal cut-outs of giant horseflies, potato beetles, mosquitoes and stink bugs. Jacques Simon defends a contrary garden when he describes his own creation at Chaumont as a 'sort of trivial provocative negative' (see p. 146).

Some examples remind us that *friche* – neglected or abandoned land – has proven a rich resource in contemporary design, though contrary to what many imagine a garden to be. Louis Benech began this series with 'Le Plaisir de la friche (The Pleasures of Wasteland) in 1992. Dutch architect Michael Van Gessel in 1995 tackled the sacred greensward by displaying a patch of thin lawn surrounded by lush meadow. The lawn partly sank under your feet as you advanced because its 'soil' was in fact was 'a light mattress of water, lined with thick felt, mineral wool, then sand.' The 'Jardin nomade' (Nomadic Garden) of 1998 suggested not the elegance of ephemeral land art, but rushed and transitory plantings, decked with worn out and recycled 'found objects' like the fishnet pergola. Trowels and saucepans collected drips resounding in mock-musical sequence.

Sometimes the whole garden is simply a joke, satirical or not. 'Y-a plus d'saisons' (1994) for example, or 'Pouf, poufs, poufs' (2001) which inverts the 'outdoor room' idea, creating living-room furniture out of plants and using giant lampshades as watering spouts. The problem with jokes in garden design is that once you get the punchline, there is little incentive to look again.

Chaumont's contrary gardens have offered a deeper challenge to conventional values. However, Frédérique Garnier's 'Jardin hostile' (Hostile Garden) of 1995 might have been planted by the devil's peasant with its rich collection of prickly, stinging and spiny plants. But its title punned on *le jardin ose-t-il?* Does the garden dare? At Chaumont it does.

nihilium

1995 Vladimir Sitta, Australia

Czech-born, Australian-based Vladimir Sitta practises
his art from Singapore to Los Angeles. His website
offers a 'sketchbook' of fantastic landscapes which
his partner, Richard Weller, an articulate spokesman
for postmodernism, links to the Western tradition of
follies and grottoes. Weller describes Sitta's 'doodles'
as 'objects with internalized dramas…simultaneously
surreal and romantic, or sublime and even ridiculous…
indulging in an artifice which is sometimes humorous,
often excessive and partially self-parody.' Like all of
Sitta's work, he comments, they reject 'post-industrial
pastoral' which Sitta has described as 'one of the
most dangerous illusions of our time.'

'Nihilium' responded to Chaumont's theme of
'Curiosity Gardens' by bringing such a doodle to life.
The wooden Cornucopia Wall rose opposite a pile
of bones. From its rounded back extended the bare,
clean roots of six *Ailanthus* trees. From the inner
curve 'leaked' long fountains of greenery – vines such
as Virginia creeper, which seemed, thanks to careful
placing, to be the luxuriant heads of the dead roots
on the other side. The greenery fell towards large
terracotta pots empty except for wood chips
preserved from the wall's jagged 'wounds', made
when the holes were pierced. Hidden inside the
metre-thick structure were other pots which in fact
held, fed and watered the thriving plants. Peepholes
with perspex tubes, lined in some cases with US
dollar notes, allowed eye-to-eye confrontation with

Opposite and right On his website, Sitta quotes the poet Baudelaire
describing street shows in Paris 'whose enormous, crude magic
subjects me to the spell of a useful illusion.' 'Nihilium' continues this
tradition, playing with spatial illusion, creating precarious balances
and dubious relationships which subjugate the viewer.

Above and right What magic goes on inside the Cornucopia Wall, so that dead *Ailanthus* roots on one side can produce thriving creeper cascades on the other? The presence of death – the roots, the bones – teases viewer sensibilities, as does the deceptively inviting piece of lawn laid over a buried water mattress.

giant cockroaches and some of the world's deadliest spiders. A metronome slowly ticked away inside.

The narrow end of the Cornucopia, roughly 'broken' off, appeared to be pierced by a wooden ladder which also penetrated an upright juniper nearby. The upper part of the ladder was coated with white chicken feathers while the bottom was bare, except for blood-red paint on the broken ends. Wild poppies grew in far corners of the plot. A poplar was tilted and tied so that it was nearly bent over double, almost touching the pile of bones. Beyond this was a small area of fresh turf, reassuring to look at but rendered unstable by a buried waterbed.

'What is actually living, what is dead?' asked the commentary, 'What is visible and invisible?' The challenge to curiosity was witty, original, perverse, more aggressive than seductive thanks to the metronome's ominous ticking, the deceptive lawn, the tortured vegetation, wounded wood and giant, distorted insects. Is the function of art to soothe or to challenge? Weller judges that 'the violence of culture acting upon the landscape is Sitta's aesthetic source' and concludes: 'This is not an easy beauty.' Baudelaire might have laughed, Virginie surely not.

Sitta's plans take into account every angle and detail, including the wild red poppies scattered in far corners to echo the red paint on the ladder, inevitably suggesting blood.

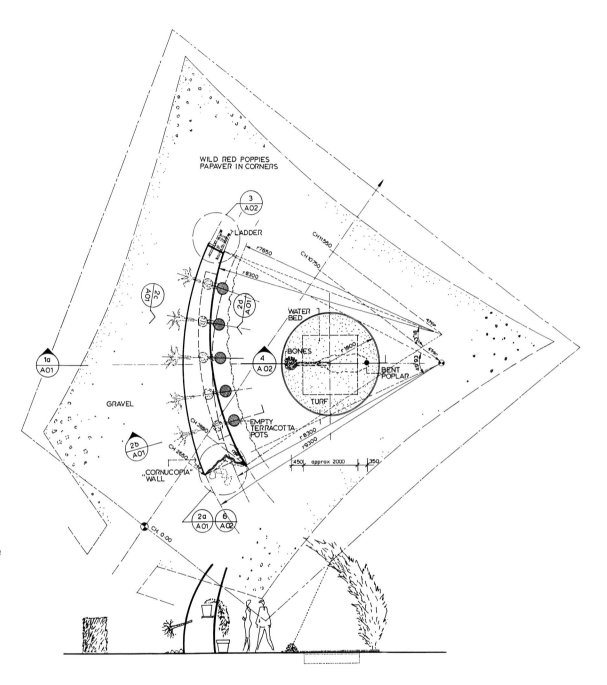

from moulds to mould: a fungus garden

de la mosaïculture vers la moisiculture 2001 Benjamin Avignon and Saweta Clouet, France

Benjamin Avignon and Saweta Clouet, French architects from Nantes, imagined an original treatment of the *mosaïculture* (carpet bedding) theme of 2001. Almost all the growth of this contrary garden was concentrated in 350 fungus specimens , a world of microclimates and miniature landscapes contained in small, round laboratory sample boxes. Their variety and colour contrasted starkly with an austere setting consisting of a translucent white tunnel set on black surfacing and surrounded by black, burnt and truncated trees. The effect was that of a kind of cocoon in which visitors had to enter to view the fungi. To heighten this impression, two cubes of lace at each end contained the evolving cocoons of real butterflies, replaced on a weekly basis, which were set among cabbages and mustard plants. Thus, the artists determined to 'discard flower beds' and reach 'less frivolous' concepts such as 'the symbolic ambiguity of life and death.'

There was much fine detailing throughout, playing with expectations of scale: the cocoon itself was made from a broad strip of the kind of Calais lace usually found only in doily dimensions. Deliberately kitsch, it had a spidery, linear Chantilly motif. White plastic stars helped to hold it in place over a metal spiral and white plastic foam provided inside support for the display. The black lead paving had similar variations in texture and pattern, imitating fossils and sometimes the actual paving stones of the city of Nantes. Outside, black rubber chips provided softer, more springy surfacing and these alternated in places with strips of grass. In the far corners were clumps of brambles and nettles.

In this black-and-white setting of dead trees and plastic, live plants included brambles, nettles and various brassicas serving as fodder to captive black and white butterflies.

Opposite left and right Austere outdoor and indoor spaces combined to entice visitors into the tunnel, there to discover life's exuberance where it was least expected. Specimen cases displaying multicoloured bacterial plant life not only surprised and sometimes delighted the eye, they also effected an unsettling change of scale in the visitors' perception.

Avignon and Clouet built the structures themselves with the help of their colleague Stéphane Roisnard and with advice from an engineering school. Specimens were provided thanks to M. Cahagnier, expert in mould cultures. The actual construction was as daring as the concept: stabilizing took place only when the cocoon was finished and its exact weight known. The creators had confidence that visitors, even if ignorant of technique, would sense both their care and their desire to open up both spaces and minds. Certainly the basic concept was easy to

grasp, and although it was disorienting and potentially hostile, the installation had an austere beauty which compelled attention and made it one of the popular successes of 2001. Avignon and Clouet recently won a government prize awarded to architects under thirty-five years of age, and participated in the 2002 French pavilion at the Venice Biennale.

Left Looking out towards the dead black forest from inside was an almost spectral experience. Every angle of vision revealed something new.

Right Spirals of white plastic stars were among the first elements constructed by the artists, who substituted these and the fungal specimens for flowers of traditional gardens.

Above The white foam tunnel was folded around its metal frame before being wrapped in Calais lace of the sort normally reserved for small accessories like dainty doilies.

Below The thin lead panels making up the path into the tunnel were sewn together like fabric, and revealed a variety of textures, like fossils.

cultivated kitsch

Taste is a favourite target of the carnival spirit, which gleefully makes fun of anything elitist. Many projects at Chaumont have satirized compulsive middle-class neatness and garden consumerism. 'La Scène du poisson' (The Fish Scene) in 2000 recreated the

aseptic 1950s-style garden parodied by Jacques Tati in his film *Mon Oncle* (My Uncle), though its creator, Christian Mallemouche, admits to a fascination with this near-cubist abstraction which he feels Tati may have shared. 'Ricochets sur l'art de vivre' (Ricochets off the Art of Living) of 1998 was a spoof on today's pretensions to gracious living. Both were strikingly graphic in a way that held attention beyond the obvious message.

The postmodern goes further, say its historians, delighting in 'excess, play, carnival, asymmetry, even mess, and in the emancipation of meanings from their bondage to mere lumpenreality'.[6] Perhaps the most striking example was made by famous scenographer Macha Makeieff, author of a work called *The Poetics of Disaster*. She and her partner Jérôme Deschamps have been creating outrageous spoofs in the theatre since 1978. In 1997 she designed 'La Fuite' for Chaumont, a title that plays on the French word for both 'leak' and 'flight'. Seemingly abandoned, a mouldy caravan was half-smothered in nettles and nasturtiums, surrounded by rusty bird cages, a clothes line and artificial plastic flowers. Brambles and nettles invaded all. Some visitors took flight.

Freud attributed the pleasure of wit to a liberation from taboos. Chaumont's very choice of themes often suggest the fun of defying middle-class conventions. Thus '*Mosaïculture* and co.' in 2001 deliberately flaunted a style now considered kitsch. Bedding geometries were once so popular that Russell Page condemned them as 'garish witnesses to a lack of invention and a slavery to custom'. What better example could there be of banality rehabilitated as art? Jean-Paul Pigeat claims that he receives more and more entries from young designers experimenting with old-fashioned plant patterning and sculpture, and often the results at Chaumont are highly original.

The 'Eroticism in the Garden' theme of 2002 also encouraged dubious explorations. Gardening's emphasis on growth and vitality can easily become a challenge to propriety. Already in 1997, Frank Herscher's magic mushrooms and cabbages were rising and deflating suggestively according to water pressure in his 'Tuyaux de Saint-Guy' (Saint Guy Hosepipes). In 1999 a fictitious Rocky Siffredo (in fact the gardeners of the Conservatoire) created 'Viagreen': after years of strict organic gardening, they produced a crop of giant vegetables 'doped' to the hilt with nitrogen. Interestingly, both the eroticism and the *mosaïculture* themes played with kitsch, but only the latter drew criticism. Could it be that bedding out offended highbrow critics because it involved social snobbery, whereas sexual vulgarity could be merely construed as politically correct permissiveness?

The potager or kitchen garden theme was also denounced as a vulgar unleashing of 'potagitis' all over the country. This term was invented by historian Monique Mosser, one of Chaumont's most virulent critics, who called the whole phenomenon 'gardenesque idiocy'. She complained: 'You put together bits of this and that, anything at all, old buckets, everyone is very happy about it, it's playful and fun' (*ludique et rigolo*). Mosser vehemently objects to the presence of humour in the gardens at Chaumont though she uses wit quite deftly herself in her attacks.[7] If Chaumont were not controversial, it would not be effective.

Right above and below Self-conscious kitsch may satirize conventional taste and garden consumerism, but it can also lead to a new sensibility, elegant in its own right. Thus, Christian Mallemouche, inspired by Jacques Tati's parodies, designed a neo-cubist fantasy entitled 'La Scène du poisson' (The Fish Scene, 2000).

Opposite 'Rendez-vous sur l'herbe' (Rendez-vous on the Grass, 1995) offered a lawn that sunk when walked on, at once upsetting visitors and their expectations.

Above The tree-trunk tool shed with its comical chimney seemed the abode of a gardener who had just stepped out – an impression heightened by the old bicycle parked by the entrance.

Right Visitors felt particularly welcome in this garden, thanks in part to a long bench made from a split log by the entrance. Many even picnicked here.

Opposite Inventive recycling involved materials such as glass bottles, snail shells, gutters and downspouts, a wooden cable drum, tyres and, by the pool, fishnet support for tomato vines.

grandad's
do-it-yourself garden

bidouille de grand-père 1999 Patrick Chappert-Gaujal,
Eric Martin and Dominique Cazal, France

Patrick Chappert-Gaujal is an artist who often makes
driftwood assemblages called 'interior landscapes'.
Eric Martin designs gardens and directs the Agence
AD, and Dominique Cazal is an architect. In 1998
they created 'Ricochets sur l'art de vivre' on the
theme of the pleasure garden, and in 1999, they
converted the same plot into 'Bidouille de grand-
père', retaining the general outline and pool. No
other team has won a place at Chaumont two years
in a row in the same way. Their combination of good
humour, inventiveness and delight proved irresistible.

   Grandad's plot welcomed visitors by providing
benches – two long tree trunks cut in half. They were
always occupied, a resting place both convenient
and inviting. A rusty bicycle leaning behind them
suggested an owner's momentary absent, perhaps
to fetch wine from the bottle-cooling niche in the
pool or to poke around in the tool shed fashioned
from a giant plane tree. With its perky, if useless, little
stovepipe, it seemed lifted straight out of a fairy tale.

   Reclaiming and recycling were a main theme of
this garden which kept well under the allotted budget.
The plot was bordered with rows of upended bottles
and strips of empty snail shells. Gutters designed to
catch roof run-off were here used as planters, raised
waist-high from the ground on supports. They made
bending easier, protected plants against ground
pests and supported crops such as red chicory,
purslane and dandelion greens, physalis and purple
amaranthus. An organ composed of zinc downspouts
provided vertical planters for carrots, turnips, broccoli,
celery – and scorzonera. A salad basket suspended
on a wire held arugula, with mirrors hanging below
to keep off the birds. Giant tin cans held chard,
aubergine, cauliflower, violets and rhubarb, each
equipped with a wick leading into water nearby.
A fig-tree planter made from a pile of old tyres had
room for a circle of parsley. A wooden cable drum

This team alone won a plot at Chaumont two years running (1998–99) for two completely different gardens. Both were tongue-in-cheek celebrations of life's colours and flavours.

Right and above Water dripped from pebble-brochettes, then flowed along a central rill to the small pool at one end, where it kept Grandad's wine bottle cool. Many rare vegetables were included in the selection including skirret and scorzonera, amaranthus 'Tricolor', plantain, perennial celery, celery root and a long list of greens.

Right The diagonal raised beds and vertical brochettes provided strong definition and direction for the eye in the midst of so much colourful exuberance.

Below Nets stretched between two existing trees beyond the basin supported tomato vines planted in rice sacks among watercress. Often ripe tomatoes had to be rescued from the water.

was turned into a cage for fasting snails. Fish netting strung between two trees supported tomato vines and upturned magnum wine bottles with the bases removed were set in a wooden rack and contained a herb garden. Another section of tree trunk was cut away to provide shelves for trailing strawberries, cherry tomatoes, sweet and hot peppers and ice plant (*Mesembryanthemum crystallinum*).

Pleasure came from the overall contemporary design with its strong diagonals and pebble-brochettes. Rather avant-garde for Grandad, these features were nonetheless perfectly adaptable to home gardens.

topiary for fun

topiaires pour rire 2001 Vannucci Piante, Jardiland and the gardeners of the Conservatoire international des parcs et jardins et du paysage, Italy and France

In 2001 the Chaumont theme of '*Mosaïculture* and co.' broke with the Festival's established preference for naturalistic plantings to explore the formal patternings which were common in late-19th-century town gardens. Topiary was encouraged as a three-dimensional variation on self-consciously artificial shape and pattern making. Contemporary garden designers in many countries are in fact reinventing this ancient technique of 'living sculpture', noted already in the 1st century BC by the natural historian Pliny the Elder who describes cypresses clipped into 'hunt scenes, fleets of ships, and all sorts of images'. The word 'topiary' derives from the Greek word *topia* meaning landscape, and for the Romans *opera topiaria* meant all kinds of ornamental gardening. As figurative plant sculpture, it proliferated in Roman villa gardens of the late empire. Revived in the 15th century in Italy, it was popular in Tuscan domains like the Villa Rucellai, admired at the time for its 'apes donkeys, oxen, bear, giants, men, women'[8] created from various evergreens on withy frames.

Later history alternates between admiration for craftsmanship and condemnations for vulgarity – the kind of ambiguity that the Chaumont organizers love to provoke. The Tuscan Vannucci Piante nursery is a leader in the field of topiary, displaying many forms at its 158-hectare site near Pistoia. Famous in particular for its mastery of climbing plants, such as ivy (*Hedera hibernica*), wisteria and vines, Vannucci uses metal structures stuffed with coconut matting to support the plants. Vannucci's experiments with privet (*Ligustrum delavayanum*) include helicopters, kayaks, the Eiffel Tower, whales and high-stepping horses.

Topiary usually stands out in formal surroundings, against lawns or gravel surfaces and dark hedging. The Chaumont team, with the help of the Jardiland company, chose to set Vannucci's fantasy figures in a luxuriant jungle. They found inspiration in the work of the artist Henri Rousseau – including no doubt the *Joyeux Farceurs* painting of 1906. At Chaumont, fish co-exist with birds, a giraffe, an elephant and a hen, while a car and cyclist pass through.

The scale is jumbled in the juxtaposition of the figures in the foliage. An exotic landscape worthy of the painter is amusingly recreated with elephants'

ears, elephants' foot (*Nolina recurvata*) variegated *codiaeum* ('Petra' and 'Banana' cultivars), Egyptian cocoa root, papyrus, agapanthus, asparagus, cycads, horsetail, fatsia and gunnera. No sharp yuccas however – one of Rousseau's favourites. No murderous attacks either, which often occur in the painter's scenes. On the contrary, visitors at Chaumont survived this garden with pleasure and appreciated it for what it was, topiary for fun.

Above and left In 2002, the menagerie moved to a wilder site close to the Festival entrance, greeting new visitors with spectral presences set against the château's turrets. New figures were added from countries all over the world, confirming Chaumont's global vocation as well as its constantly irreverent spirit of fun and fancy.

Opposite Italian topiary figures inhabited a décor inspired by the paintings of the Douanier Rousseau – including no doubt the *Joyeux Farceurs* of 1906.

flights of fancy

Chaumont's greatest value lies in being what critic Murielle Hucliez calls 'a laboratory for the imagination' (*laboratoire de la fantaisie*).[9] This is where postmodern irony gives way to the pure play of Baudelaire's 'absolute comic'. The eroticism theme was also an assertion of vitality, a contemporary reply to the Thanatos of land art's early days. In the intervening decades, gardens have become a privileged forum for these explorations, for what are gardens if not an affirmation of life forces?

'Entre épingles' (Among Hatpins, 2001) exhibited a forest of 'hatpins' rising from a white 'veil', each globe planted with dark red sedums and topped with a palm feather.

So at Chaumont the delight of children is after all part of paradise. Flowers laugh when you touch them, the Three Little Pigs of the fairy tale grow their own vegetables, robots turn somersaults, miniature island gardens dance downstream, pumpkins fly and snails race, spotted hatpins float over vaporous floral chiffon, dragon flies emerge between the boards you are standing on and the weeping of the baobab turns into an abundance of never-fading blooms.

In 'Mosaïculture aquatique' (Aquatic Bedding, 2001), a water parterre displayed fish instead of flowers and artificial flowers in the aquariums, all set among curving mirrors and centred on a crystal fountain.

puddle reflection

réflexion dans une flaque d'eau 2001 Serge Mansau
and Michel Cabornac for Yves Rocher, France

Serge Mansau has been sculpting glass for thirty years, creating everything from cabins or huts of layered leaves to vials for precious perfumes: diamonds for Cartier's 'Declaration', scintillating draperies for Givenchy's 'Organza', others still for Kenzo, Lancôme, Cerruti and Christian Dior. Some of his models bear the imprint of a leaf, bark or roots collected during walks around his country home outside Paris. The forest there is inhabited by fauna of his making, including several centaurs. Nature has always provided inspiration for him but he avoids direct imitation, filtering impressions through dream and memory. Mansau particularly likes to work with glass because it captures light and mirrors the movements of wind and water.

In 2001 the cosmetics firm Yves Rocher asked him to collaborate on a project for Chaumont. Mansau had been dreaming of participating for years and presented three suggestions to Jean-Paul Pigeat, whom he describes as 'a gigantic, elusive personality, at once enthusiastic and inspirational'. Instead of choosing one entry, Pigeat accepted all three – a first at the Festival. Mansau's main contribution was 'Réflexion dans une flaque d'eau'. The Yves Rocher company, which sponsors famous public gardens in Brittany, provided the help of their plantsman Michel Cabornac.

Vincent van Gogh admired Japanese painters who could find a whole world in a blade of grass. Mansau imagined a giant puddle 197 feet (60 metres) across on which slender 'leaves' seemed to float, with others barely visible at the bottom of the shallow water. A viewing platform ran along one side by the entrance. Only from one angle was the illusion complete and extended by the glinting of the Loire river beyond. In this very linear composition, everything converged on a rising glass sculpture of frosted leaves over which water cascaded back into the pool. Now and then, mists wafted up as from a pond in autumn, fragrant clouds smelling of moss and wood which further enhanced the shimmering of the glass and water.

Many visitors compared the leaves to boats – gondolas or dug-out canoes. And indeed in an

accompanying poem, Mansau made the metaphor explicit: 'I have kept from a nomadic childhood dozens of small boxes containing incredible worlds all in a walnut shell…tremendous marine battles fought with bamboo leaves on a mere puddle…'. At Chaumont, the artist perceived his larger-than-life landscape as 'a snapshot taken in the heat of the action, reassembling not only colours and shapes but instants, fragments of time and of everyday being.'

Mansau captured a childhood fantasy at the instant when leaves half float, half sink, into water. On this giant scale, they also resemble the 'drunken boats' which inspired the French poet Rimbaud.

Low-growing shrubs chosen for colour and texture included *Berberis thunbergii* 'Bonanza Gold', *Cotoneaster procumbens* 'Streib's Findling', *Lonicera nitida* 'Baggesen's Gold', *Deutzia crenata* 'Nikko', ivies and junipers.

Left Mansau's glass sculpture is often shown in Parisian galeries. The central focal point of this vision remained his glass-leaf fountain scintillating among scented autumn mists.

green phantasy landscape: encounter with verner panton

2002 Grégorie Reynès-Dutertre, Philippe Dutertre, Arnauld Delacroix, Patrick de Bruyn, France and Denmark

The Danish architect Verner Panton was among the first to create integral environments in which he controlled every detail of the design. His colours were flamboyant, his shapes futuristic. In the 1960s he produced the legendary Panton chair from a single piece of moulded plastic. Reissued today by Habitat, Innovation Randers of Denmark and Vitra, it symbolizes a Panton revival which is also evident in current museum interest. Vitra's 2001 exhibition recreated Panton's famous 'Phantasy Landscape', first revealed in 1970 at the Visiona 2 design show

Left The famous Panton chair made from a single piece of moulded plastic was present here as a row of shocking pink seats just visible from the garden's entrance, inviting further exploration.

Opposite The design evolved in a semi-enclosed space which grew shadier as the season progressed. But in keeping with the 2002 eroticism theme, voyeurism was encouraged from outside.

Above Climbers included cobea, moon vine, honeysuckle, periwinkle, lace vine, runner beans and several clematis (*C. alionushka*, *C. x eriostemon*, *C.flammula*, *C. gouriana* and *C. x jouiniana* 'Praecox').

in Cologne. This was a kind of box interior which critic Marc Spiegler called a 'psychedelic love-fest setting'.[10] Entered through porthole-shaped doors at either end, the exhibit provided 'sitting spaces, shoulder-height outcroppings to lean on, and low, level areas fit for a long nap…unexpected and organic forms' easily conducive, according to observers, to sexual experimentation.

The architect Grégorie Reynès-Dutertre admired this exhibit in Basel and remembered it when considering Chaumont's 2002 eroticism theme. Could Panton's seductive box be translated into garden greenery? Might this structure allow some intimacy at a festival where thousands pass by daily? With the support of Panton's widow and Philippe, her partner, Grégorie teamed up with sculptor Patrick de Bruyn to copy the exact proportions and internal structures of Panton's original design. They replaced Panton's fabrics with metal mesh, triply and pink and black wood chips. They added a row of Panton chairs outside to allow comparison of forms, but also to give visitors a chance to 'savour the moment' in quiet reflection. The plantsman and designer Arnauld Delacroix provided an elegant jungle of climbing plants both within and without. Grégorie felt that their filtered light and shade transcribed Panton's colour contrasts, while Arnauld remembered Romantic garden follies, trysts, false ruins and plants running wild. Thus a hedgerow honeysuckle wafted its pervasive scent through the webbed furnishings and, by the opening day, faithful lace vine (*Polygonum aubertii*) had scaled the heights to begin flowering. Overall, blooms were deliberately discrete – mainly in white or blue – with only one clematis to echo Panton's shocking pinks.

The 'adult funhouse' quality that Spiegler attributes to much of Panton's work was softened but not subdued. This critic considers that the 'retro wave has been cloaked in deep irony, a sentiment completely absent from Panton's creations. With hindsight on the decades of greed that followed, it's easy to mock his work's exuberance and idealism. But it's just as easy to envy it.' 'Green Phantasy Landscape' was elegiac rather than ironic, a moment of pleasure offered and taken.

notes

Extracts not referenced here are either to be found easily
in the Bibliography p. 190 or are taken from live interviews
and personal correspondence with the author. Full details of
works given in short-title form will be found in the Bibliography.
World Wide Web references are given as they appeared
at the time of going to press.

The Chaumont Story

1 For exact details, see the List of Gardens p. 185 or
the Chaumont website with its year-by-year presentation
of gardens at www.chaumont-jardins.com.

2 Stephen Anderton, 'Carpet Bedding', *Gardens Illustrated*,
May 2002, p. 22.

3 Pigeat, *Les Jardins du futur*, p 23.

4 Quoted in the Chaumont press release for 2002.

5 Aude Charié, Agence Papyrus, 3 passage du Grand Cerf,
75002 Paris, France Tel. 01 55 34 96 60 Fax 01 55 34 96
61, email papyrus.r.media@wanadoo.fr. For the designer flea
market, see www.pucesdudesign.com.

6 Guillaume Sonnet (owner), Le Vallon du Villaret, Le Hameau
du Villaret, Allenc, 48190 Bagnol-les-Bains, France,
Tel. 04 66 47 62 89, Fax 04 66 47 63 83. See also
www.capnemo.fr/vallon and the description in Jones,
The French Country Garden.

7 Le Dantec, Jean-Pierre *Le Sauvage et le régulier: Art des
jardins et paysagisme en France au XIXe siècle*, Paris,
2002, p 243.

1 Global Ties

1 Richard Weller, quoted on the agency website
www.room413.com.au.

2 Kathryn Gustafson in her preface to Amidon, *Radical
Landscapes*.

3 Péchère, *Jardins dessinés*. Quotation from France Rossignol
in personal correspondence.

4 Centre Terre Vivante, Domaine de Raud, B.P. 20, Mens,
38711 Isère, France. Tel. 04 76 34 80 80,
Fax 04 76 34 84 02. See Clément, *Thomas et le voyageur*.

5 Others include *The Postage Stamp Garden Book* by Duane
Newcomb, Los Angeles, Calif., and New York, 1975. This
approach was particularly encouraged in the publications
of the Rodale Press in Pennsylvania which founded *Organic
Gardening Magazine*, and those of *Sunset Gardening
Magazine* on the west coast.

2 What Plants Can Do

1 Patrick Blanc, *Un Peu de botanique* written for Pascal Héni
and reproduced on a compact disc recorded in Paris,
4 December 2000 during a live concert at the Hôtel de
Bondeville.

2 The CIRAD website address is www.cirad.fr.

3 Bois, Désiré, and A. Pailleux, *Le Potager d'un curieux*,
Marseilles, 1892 (reprint 1993).

4 Ossart and Maurières, *Jardins nomades et tapis de fleurs*,
p 3. English translation by Ossart and Maurières in the original
book.

5 Quoted in a review by Robert Schäfer of Kienast,
Kienast-Gardens, appearing in *Land Forum*,
Spring–Summer 1998.

6 This quotation provides the opening words of the biography
featured on Robert Wilson's own website at
www.robertwilson.com.

7 Quoted in the MASS MoCa online exhibition catalogue
for Robert Wilson's *14 Stations*, Station 5, 2002.

8 Pigeat, *Les Jardins du futur*, p 123.

3 Outdoor Art

1 Wallace Stevens, 'The Anecdote of the Jar', first published
in 1919. To see a selection of critical interpretations of this
poem, consult the website
www.english.uiuc.edu/maps/poets/s_z/stevens/jar.htm.

2 Richard Long, *Walking in Circles*, London, 1991, quoted
in Weilacher, *Between Landscape Architecture and Land Art*,
p 16.

3 Richard Weller, quoted on the agency website
www.room413.com.au.

4 Irwin, *Double Diamond*, quoted in Tiberghien, *Nature, art,
paysage*. Originally published as 'Change, Inquiry, Qualities,
Conditional', *Being and circumstance*, Santa Monica and
San Francisco, Calif., 1986.

5 Cooper and Taylor, *Gardens for the Future*, p. 178. See also
Mirrors of Paradise: The Gardens of Fernando Caruncho.

6 Amidon, *Radical Landscapes*, p. 31.

4 Time and Change

1 Walter de Maria, cited in Weilacher, *Between Landscape
Architecture and Land Art*, p 21.

2 Robert Smithson, cited in Weilacher, *Between Landscape
Architecture and Land Art*, p 17.

3 Gilles Clément, 'La Friche apprivoisée', *Urba*, September
1985, p 95.

4 Hugh Johnson, 'Time and The Place', *The Garden*, October
2001, p 751.

5 Maurières and Ossart, *Jardins nomades*, p. 6.

6 Peter Latz, website presentation at the agency address
www.latzundpartner.de.

7 Described in detail in Corbin, *L'Homme dans le paysage*,
p. 29.

8 Peter Walker with Cathy Deino Blake, 'Minimalist Gardens
without Walls' in Francis and Hester, *The Meaning of
Gardens*, pp. 120–30.

5 The Landscape Question

1 Amidon, *Radical Landscapes*, pp. 116–19.

2 Hunt, *Greater Perfections*, p 77.

3 All quotations here are from the fuller description
of the Chaumont project found on Hargreaves's website
at www.hargreaves.com.

4 See *The Garden Book* and contributions by Potteiger and
Purington, Cooper and Douglas, Weilacher, Tiberghien.

5 See Simon, *Tous Azimuts*.

6 Interview with Keiichi Tahara by Stéphanie Michut, November
1999, cited on the website of the Courtoisie Galerie Baudoin
Lebon, Paris, www.galerie-vrais-reves.com.

7 Rainer Maria Rilke, 'Heureux les vents qui fuient vers les
jardins', in *Le Livre de la pauvreté et de la mort*, Lausanne,
1941. English translation author's own. Originally published
as *Das Stunden-Buch. Von der Armuth und vom Tode*,
Lausanne, 1941.

8 Hunt, *Greater Perfections*, pp. 79ff.

6 Wit and Whimsy

1 One exception is the account given in Maitland and
Matthews, *Gardens of Illusion*.

2 Ian McHarg, 'Nature is More than a Garden' in Francis and
Hester, *The Meaning of Gardens*, pp 34–38.

3 One set of definitions supplied by Tim O'Sullivan, John
Hartley, Danny Saunders, Martin Montgomery and John Fisk
(eds), *Key Concepts in Communication and Cultural Studies*,
New York, 1994 (2nd edition), p. 234.

4 Charles Dard on the 'Métropolitains' radio programme,
directed by François Chaslin, France Culture, 30 May 2001.

5 Pagnol, Marcel, *Jean de Florette,* Paris, 1962
(W. E. van Heyningen, trans., *The Water of the Hills:
Two Novels by Marcel Pagnol*, Berkeley, Calif., and London,
1988).

6 See note 3 above.

7 Monique Mosser 'Le XXIe siècle sera jardinier', *Le Jardin,
notre double: sagesse et déraison*, Paris, 1999, and
comments broadcast on the 'Métropolitains' radio
programme, France Culture, in an interview with François
Chaslin, 16 May 2001: *donc on fait de petits bouts, n'importe
quoi, on met de vieux seaux, enfin tout le monde est très
content de tout ça, c'est ludique et rigolo.*

8 Cited by Geoffrey and Susan Jellicoe, Patrick Goode and
Michael Lancaster in *The Oxford Companion to Gardens*,
Oxford, 1986.

9 Marielle Hucliez, *Jardins et parcs contemporains*, Paris,
1998, p. 11.

10 Marc Spiegler, 'Panton's Plastic Universe', review of Verner
Panton exhibition, 5 February–12 June 2000, Vitra Design
Museum, Weil-am-Rhein, Germany.

list of gardens

Gardens are arranged by chapter and include those cited in the text or appearing in illustrations.
To see a list of gardens by year, consult the Chaumont Festival website at: www.chaumont-jardins.com
For contact information for those involved in the main examples featured, see p. 188 or consult the CIPJP (address p. 188). Translations of the garden titles have been provided in brackets.

The Chaumont Story
'Mosaïculture aquatique' (Aquatic Bedding) 2001 Jean-Louis Cura, Marc Félix, Michèle Schneider
'Saules tressées' (Woven Willows) 1995–96 and 'Saules dans la brume' (Willows in the Mist) 1997 David and Judy Drew
'La Terre en marche' (The Earth in Motion) 1996 George Hargreaves
'Power Plants' 1993 Peter Walker
'New England Garden' (Jardin de la Nouvelle Angleterre) 1994 Lynden B. Miller
'Un Jardin clair' (A Light Garden) 1993 Susan Child
'Jardin de graminées' (Garden of Grasses) 1994 Bob Wilson and Mark Rudkin
'Desert Sea', 'Glass Garden' 2001–2002 Andy Cao and Stephen Jerrom
'L'Archipel' (The Archipelago) 1993+, Shodo Suzuki
'Eléments naturels' (Natural Elements) 1993 Haruto Kobayashi
'Tunnel de bambous' 1992, 'Bambous' 1993 (Bamboo Tunnel) Hiroshi Teshigahara
'A L'Ombre d'une gloriette' 1992 (In the Shadow of a Gloriette), La Gloriette 1993 (The Gloriette) Fernando Caruncho
'Nihilium' ('Curiosity Garden' in Chaumont listings) 1995 Room 4.1.3., Vladimir Sitta
'Jardin des os' (Bricks, Bones and Pumpkins) 2000 Adriaan Geuze
'La Fontaine de Rouchka' 1992, 'Cascade de seaux' (Bucket Waterfall) 1993 Michel Desvigne and Christine Dalnoky
'Le Plaisir de la friche' (Wasteland Pleasure) 1992 Louis Benech
'La Faute de l'Abbé Mouret' (Father Mouret's Fault) 1992 Laure Quoniam
'Rapsodie en bleu' (Rhapsody in Blue) 1995 Jacques Simon
'La Serre exotique' (The Exotic Greenhouse) 1997 'La Serre molle' (The Soft Greenhouse) 1998 'La Serre au papillons' (The Butterfly Greenhouse) 1999 Atelier de l'Entrepôt: Edouard François and Duncan Lewis
'La Yourte' (The Glass Globe) 2001 Serge Mansau
'Erotica: les chemins de la séduction' (Erotica: The Ways of Seduction) 2002 Julia Barton
'Jardin de murs végétaux' (Living Walls) 1994–97 Patrick Blanc and Michel Mangematin
'Le Jardin permanent' (Permanent Garden) 1998+ Bernard Wolgensinger
'Cour de la ferme' (Farmyard) 1994+ Eric Ossart
'La Déclaration d'amour' (The Declaration of Love) 2002 students of the Conservatoire

'Un Simple jardin d'ouvrier' (A Simple Allotment) 1992 Simone Kroll
'Trognes' (Pollards) 1999–2000 Dominique Mansion
'Code naturel' (Nature's Code) 2000 pep Studio: Katharina Schütze, Uwe Müller and Jürgen Stellwag
'Potager portugais' (Portuguese Garden) 1999 Felicia and Teresa Louart, France Rossignol
'Jardin de paille' (Straw Hut Garden) 2000 Hugues Peuvergne
'Edicules' (Conveniences) 1993+ Hélène Buisson

1 Global Ties
'Desert Sea', 'Glass Garden' 2001–2002 Andy Cao and Stephen Jerrom
'La Serre exotique' (The Exotic Greenhouse) 1997 'La Serre molle' (The Soft Greenhouse) 1998 'La Serre au papillons' (The Butterfly Greenhouse) 1999 Atelier de l'Entrepôt: Edouard François and Duncan Lewis
'Trognes' (Pollards) 1999–2000 Dominique Mansion
'Houblon: dans tous les sens' (Hop: In Every Way) 1996 Nord-Sud Paysages, Nico Bouts and Pascale Gaucher

World Tour
'Potager portugais' (Portuguese Garden) 1999 Felicia and Teresa Louart, France Rossignol
'Jardin congolais' (Congolese Garden), 'Jardin africain' (African Garden) 1999 France Rossignol inspired by René Péchère
'Potager impérial chinois', 'Jardin chinois' (Imperial Chinese Garden) 1999 Shun-Bao Du, Bin Hu Zhang and Hai Qian Zen
'Bipergorria' (Red Pepper) 2000 Ecole d'architecture et de paysage de Bordeaux: Vincent Abadie and Maïté Fourcade
'Houblon: dans tous les sens' (Hop: In Every Way) 1996 Nord-Sud Paysages, Nico Bouts and Pascale Gaucher
'TarPot' (Tartan Potager) 1999 Lumir Soukup, Nigel Buchan and Frazer McNaughton
'New England Garden' (Jardin de la Nouvelle Angleterre) 1994 Lynden B. Miller

Skills and Inventions
'Jardin de terre' (Earth Garden) 1994–95 Atelier Kaba (Team Zoo)
'Sillon romand' (Swiss Furrow) 1996 Daniel Örtli and the city of Lausanne
'Trognes' (Pollards) 1999–2000 Dominique Mansion
'La Rizière' (The Rice Paddy) 1997 Eric Ossart and students from the Ecole méditerranéenne des jardins et du paysage de Grasse
'Passerelle dans la jungle' (Jungle Footbridge) 1996 Harold Schmitt and Yves Dupont
'Folles Ipomées' (Mad Ipomoea), 'Radeau des Cimes' (Treetop Raft) 1996 Patrick Blanc and Gilles Ebersolt
'Mignonne, allons voir si la rosée…' (Darling, Let Us See If The Dew) 1998 Jacques Sordoillet, Annie Sottil and Véronique Martinez

'La Serre exotique' (The Exotic Greenhouse) 1997 'La Serre molle' (The Soft Greenhouse) 1998 'La Serre au papillons' (The Butterfly Greenhouse) 1999 Atelier de l'Entrepôt: Edouard François and Duncan Lewis
'Gardens for Bangladesh' 1999 Helen Keller International, France
'A Quoi sert ce jardin, ce jardin sert aqua?' (What is a Garden For?) 1995, 'Lagugnages' (Lagoonings) 1996 Atelier Traverses
'L'Art du potager en carrés' (Square Foot Gardening) 1999 Jean-Paul Collaert and Jean-Michel Wilmotte
'Murs de Palestine' (Walls of Palestine) 2000–2002 Bruno Marmiroli, Walid azme al-Houmouze, Patrick Genty, Veronica Alcacer

Fusion Gardens
'Mé-tissage' 1999 Eve Girardot, Laeticia Anglade and Sophie Breuil
'Mappemonde' (Garden of the World) 1994 Blumeninsel botanical gardens of Mainau
'Gaspatio andaluz' (Gaspacho) 1999 In Situ Agency: Emmanual Jalbert, Annie Tardivon, Mahaut Michez, Laurence Delorenzi, Frédéric Reynaud
'Desert Sea' ('Glass Garden') 2001–2002 Andy Cao and Stephen Jerrom

2 What Plants Can Do
'Le Jardin oriental' (The Oriental Garden) 1998 'Ô de Fleurs' 1999 (Scents and Sense) Rachid Koraïchi and Eric Ossart
'Primeval Perspective', 'New Zealand Garden' 2000 Avant Gardener agency: James Fraser and Tina Febrey
'Zingibérales' (Zingiberales) 1995 Eric Ossart and Patrick Blanc
'India Song' 1999 Eric Ossart and Patrick Blanc
'Un Jardin de fougères géantes' (Giant Fern Garden) 1995 Pépinières Yves Dupont

Botany and Biodiversity
'Un Jardin de pépiniériste' (A Nurseryman's Garden) 1994 Pépinières Maymou
'Jardin de Lagerstroemia' (Lagerstroemia Garden) 1995 Pépinières Desmartis
'Le Bassin des nymphéas' (The Water Lily Pond) 1994 'Le Jardin aquatique' (The Water Garden) 1995 'Le Bassin des nymphéas' 1996 Pépinières Latour-Marliac
'Jardin de murs végétaux' (Living Walls) 1994–97 Patrick Blanc and Michel Mangematin
'Retour de Valdivia' (Return from Valdivia) 1994 Patrick Blanc
'Folles Ipomées' (Mad Ipomoea), 'Radeau des Cimes' (Treetop Raft) 1996 Patrick Blanc and Gilles Ebersolt
'Amafas', 'Le Jardin d'amafas' (The Amafas Garden) 2001 CIRAD (Centre de coopération internationale en recherche agronomique pour le développement) and Patrick Blanc
'Le Potager d'un curieux' (Garden for a Hungry Spirit) 1999 Jean-Luc Danneyrolles

Storytelling

'Le Réveil de la tortue' (The Turtle Awakens) 2001 Alexandra Bonnin and Conservatoire gardeners

'Fier comme un paon' (Proud as a Peacock) 2001 city of Epinal

'India Song' 1999 Eric Ossart and Patrick Blanc

'Le Déluge' (The Deluge) 1998 Ecole d'architecture de paysage de l'Université de Montréal: Edith Julien, Mélanie Mignault and Michel Langevin

'Jardin et industrie' (Garden and Industry) 1994 Stefan Tischer

'Passage', 'Jardin de passage' (Garden of Passage) 1997–98 Jean-Pierre Delettre

'Le Jardin flou' (Soft and Loose) Pernilla Magnusson, Arola Tous, Silvia Vespasiani, Sara Dauge, Luís Bisbe and Alex Aguilar

'Les Pétales du désir' (The Petals of Desire) 2002 Eric-Pierre Ménard, Chantal Dugave, Franck Franjou and Aude Franjou

'Erotica: les chemins de la séduction' (Erotica: The Ways of Seduction) 2002 Julia Barton

'From Sky to Earth' 1997–99 Fumiaki Takano, Saido Higuchi, Nobushisa Inuma, from Takano Landscape Japan; Takano Landscape Taiwan; Hiroshi Naruse, Naoki Sakan, Naoki Kusumi, Mori from the Atelier Kaba

'Jardin des os' (Bricks, Bones and Pumpkins) 2000 Adriaan Geuze

'Power Plants' 1993 Peter Walker

5 The Landscape Question

'La Terre en marche' (The Earth in Motion) 1996 George Hargreaves

'Vallon des brumes' (Misty Vale) 2000+ Conservatoire gardeners

'Désert noir auvergnat' (Black Auvergne Desert) 1994, 'Des Cactées pour le désert' (Desert Cacti) 1995 Bernard Wolgensinger

'La Rizière' (The Rice Paddy) 1997 Eric Ossart and students from the Ecole méditerranéenne des jardins et du paysage de Grasse

Games with Scale

'La Rizière' (The Rice Paddy) 1997 Eric Ossart and students from the Ecole méditerranéenne des jardins et du paysage de Grasse

'Murs de Palestine' (Walls of Palestine) 2000–2002 Bruno Marmiroli, Walid azme al-Houmouze, Patrick Genty and Veronica Alcacer

'New England Garden' (Jardin de la Nouvelle Angleterre) 1994 Lynden B. Miller

'La Côte d'Azur' (A Mediterranean Garden) 1994 Jean Mus

'Réflexion dans une flaque d'eau' (Puddle Reflection) 2001 Serge Mansau

'Barbibulle' (Barbibubble) 1997 Ecole nationale supérieure de la nature et du paysage de Blois

'Les Enfants dans l'eau' (Children in Water) 1997 Pro Urba and Conservatoire gardeners

'La Ménagerie était trempée' (The Menagerie Was Soaked) 1998–99 Pro Urba and Conservatoire gardeners

'Ivre de la jungle' (Jungle Drunk) 2000 Pro Urba and Conservatoire gardeners

'Potager en l'île' (Island Potager) 1994 Agence Européenne du paysage: Bernard Chapuis and Georges Vafias

'Jardin de murs végétaux' (Living Walls) 1994–97 Patrick Blanc and Michel Mangematin

'Pampa, vers l'infini par la monotonie' (The Pampas: from Monotony to Infinity) Martina Barzi and Josefina Casares 2001–2002

Symbolic Landscapes

'L'Archipel' (The Archipelago) 1993+, Shodo Suzuki

'Désert noir auvergnat' (Black Auvergne Desert) 1994, 'Des Cactées pour le désert' (Desert Cacti) 1995 Bernard Wolgensinger

'Trognes' (Pollards) 1999–2000 Dominique Mansion

'Sillon romand' (Swiss Furrow) 1996 Daniel Örtli and the city of Lausanne

'Mente la menta?' (Does the Mint Lie?) 2000 Land-I Agency: Marco Antonini, Roberto Capecci and Raffaella Sini

'Code naturel' (Nature's Code) 2000 pep Studio: Katharina Schütze, Uwe Müller and Jürgen Stellwag

'La Terre en marche' (The Earth in Motion) 1996 George Hargreaves

'Rapsodie en bleu' (Rhapsody in Blue) 1995 Jacques Simon

Context

'Mouvements de Loire' (The Flowing Loire) 2001 Ville de Tours: Daniel Jud and Philippe Herlin

'Vallon des brumes' (Misty Vale) 2000+ Conservatoire gardeners

'Lointain extérieur' (View Beyond) 1993 Atelier Phusis: Marc Claramunt, Christophe Girot and Jean-Marc L'Anton

'Le Triangle d'eau' (The Water Triangle) 1998 Keiichi Tahara

'Sentier de fers sauvages' (Wild Iron Path) 1998+ Jean Lautrey

6 Wit and Whimsy

'Topiaires pour rire', 'Topiaires à l'italienne' (Topiary for Fun) 2001 Vanucci Piante, Jardiland and Conservatoire gardeners

'Le Baobab qui pleure' (The Weeping Baobab) 1997+ Edouard Boulmier, François Kiéné and Conservatoire staff

'La Fuite' (Leaky Escape) 1997 Macha Makeieff

'Trois cabanes' (Three Huts) 1999 Marc Soucat and Jean-Marc Bourry

Contrary Gardens

'Le Jardin hostile – Le Jardin ose-t-il?' (The Hostile Garden – Does the Garden Dare?) 1995 Frédérique Garnier

'Potager nomade' (Nomadic Kitchen Garden) 1999 Patrick Nadeau, Vincent Dupont-Rougier and Joëlle Alexandre

'Trampoline' 1998 Michael Blier

'Centre d'accueil pour les nuisibles' (Welcome Centre for Pests) 1993 Gérald and Geneviève Poussin

'Rapsodie en bleu' (Rhapsody in Blue) 1995 Jacques Simon

'Le Plaisir de la Friche' (Wasteland Pleasure) 1992 Louis Benech

'Rendez-vous sur l'herbe' (Rendez-vous on the Grass) 1995 Michael Van Gessel

'Jardin nomade' (Nomadic Garden) 1998 Alessandro Escher and Laura Stella Morellini

'Y'a plus d'saisons' (No More Seasons) 1994 Atelier Ephémère

'Pouf, pouf, pouf' 2001 Nathalie Leroy and Renaud Paque

'Nihilium' ('Curiosity Garden' in Chaumont listings) 1995 Room 4.1.3., Vladimir Sitta

'De la Mosaïculture vers la moisiculture' (From Moulds to Mould) 2001 Benjamin Avignon and Saweta Clouet

Cultivated Kitsch

'Rendez-vous sur l'herbe' (Rendez-vous on the Grass) 1995 Michael Van Gessel

'La Scène du poisson' (The Fish Scene) 2000 Christian Mallemouche

'Ricochets sur l'art de vivre' (Ricochets off the Art of Living) 1998 Patrick Chappert-Gaujal, Eric Martin and Dominique Cazal

'La Fuite' (The Leaky Escape) 1997 Macha Makeieff

'Les Tuyaux de Saint Guy' (Saint Guy Hosepipes) 1997 Frank Herscher

'Viagreen' 1999 Rocky Siffredo (pseudonym for Conservatoire gardeners)

'Bidouille de grand-père' (Grandad's Do-It-Yourself Garden) 1999 Patrick Chappert-Gaujal, Eric Martin and Dominique Cazal

'Topiaires pour rire', 'Topiaires à l'italienne' (Topiary for Fun) 2001 Vanucci Piante, Jardiland and Conservatoire gardeners

Flights of Fancy

'Entre épingles' (Among Hatpins) 2001 Levin Monsigny, Luc Monsigny, Axel Hermening, Nicoali Levin and Marina Levin

'Mosaïculture aquatique' (Aquatic Bedding) 2001 Jean-Louis Cura, Marc Félix, Michèle Schneider

'Le Jardin extraordinaire' (The Extraordinary Garden) 2000 Jean-Brice Moirgeat

'Le Potager dansant' (The Dancing Potager) 1998 Students of the Conservatoire

'Trajectoire' (Trajectory) 1999 Christophe Camfrancq, Guido Fanti and Catherine Champenois

'La Course aux escargots' (The Snail Race) 2001 Yvan Dayan, Emmanuel Prieur and France Yvan Dayan

'Le Jardin qui rit' (The Laughing Garden) 1995 Véronique Krieff and Gail Wittwer

'Trois cabanes' (Three Huts) 1999 Marc Soucat and Jean-Marc Bourry

'Le Salon flottant' (The Floating Lounge) 2000 Laurent Romanet

'Réflexion dans une flaque d'eau' (Puddle Reflection) 2001 Serge Mansau

'Green Phantasy Landscape: An Encounter with Verner Panton' 2002 Grégorie Reynès-Dutertre, Philippe Dutertre, Arnauld Delacroix and Patrick de Bruyn

contact details

For those involved in the main gardens featured in the book, listed in order of appearance. See p. 185 for a list of other gardens mentioned or illustrated. Contact information for these can be obtained from the CIPJP (listed below).

Jean-Paul Pigeat, Director
Conservatoire international des
 Parcs et Jardins et du Paysage
 (CIPJP)
Ferme du château
41150 Chaumont-sur-Loire
France
T +33 (0)2 54 20 99 22
F +33 (0)2 54 20 99 24
E cipjp.documentation@wanadoo.fr
www.chaumont-jardins.com
or
CIPJP
12 rue Brisemiche
75004 Paris
France
T +33 (0)1 48 04 84 59
F +33 (0)1 42 71 54 46
E cipjp.paris@wanadoo.fr

1 Global Ties

World Tour

Tartan Potager TarPot 1999

Lumir Soukup
53/7 East Crosscauseway
Edinburgh, EH8 9HD
Scotland
T +44 (0)131 668 4037
E lumirsoukup@hotmail.com

Frazer McNaughton
E frazer.mcnaughton@snh.gov.uk

Nigel Buchan
E nigel.buchan@snh.gov.uk

New England Garden 1994

Lynden B. Miller
1170 Fifth Avenue
New York City
NY10029
USA
T +1 212 722 5497
F +1 212 534 5314
E LBMtilia@aol.com

Skills and Inventions

Square Foot Gardening
 L'Art du potager en carrés
 1999

Jean Paul Collaert
Gazette des jardins
23 avenue du Parc Robiony
06200 Nice
France
T +33 (0)4 93 96 16 13
F +33 (0)4 92 15 00 61
E lgi@wanadoo.fr

Jean-Michel Wilmotte & Associés
68 rue du Faubourg Saint Antoine
75012 Paris
France
T +33 (0)1 53 02 22 22
F +33 (0)1 43 44 17 11
E wilmotte@wanadoo.fr

Walls of Palestine
 Murs de Palestine
 2000–2002

L'Atelier: Bruno Marmiroli,
 Walid azme al-Houmouze,
 Patrick Genty, Veronica Alcacer
2 Impasse de la Forge
37460 Céré La Ronde
France
T +33 (0)2 47 94 38 30
F +33 (0)2 47 94 30 55
E Latelier@worldonline.fr

Fusion Gardens

Gaspacho
 Gaspatio andaluz 1999

Agence In Situ:
Emmanual Jalbert, Annie Tardivon,
Mahaut Michez, Laurence
Delorenzi, Frédéric Reynaud
30 quai Saint Vincent
69001 Lyon
France
T +33 (0)4 78 30 50 15
F +33 (0)4 72 07 07 72
E contact@in-situ.fr
www.in-situ.fr

Desert Sea 2001–2002

Andy Cao & Stephen Jerrom
Glass Garden, Inc.

3511 West 6th Street, Studio 17
Los Angeles
CA 90020
USA
T +1 213 368 9220
F +3 368 9226
E info@landscape2go.com
www.glassgardendesign.com

2 What Plants Can Do

Botany and Biodiversity

Amafas Jardin d'amafas 2001

CIRAD: Centre de coopération
 internationale en recherche
 agronomique pour le
 développement
42 rue Scheffer
75116 Paris
France
T +33 (0)1 53 70 20 00
F +33 (0)1 47 55 15 30
www.cirad.fr

Patrick Blanc
111 rue du Général Leclerc
94000 Créteil
France
T +33 (0)1 42 07 59 95
F +33 (0)1 48 99 86 21

Garden for a Hungry Spirit
 Le Potager d'un curieux 1999

Jean-Luc Danneyrolles
'Le Potager d'un curieux'
La Molière
84400 Saignon
France
T +33 (0)4 90 74 44 68

Sensuous Gardening

Scents and Sense
 Ô de Fleurs 1998
Rachid Koraïchi
36 rue du Colonel Pierre Avia
75015 Paris
France
T/F +33 (0)1 40 60 68 94

Eric Ossart and Arnaud Maurières
Avenue Paul Bodin
81190 Tanus
France

T +33 (0)5 63 76 38 49
F +33 (0)5 63 76 47 06
E ossart-maurieres@wanadoo.fr

Soft and Loose
 Le Jardin flou 2002

Alex Aguilar
E ultraverde@eresmas.com

Luis Bisbe
E l.bisbe@mailcity.com

Sara Dauge
E sara@bethgali.com

Pernilla Magnusson
E pernilla@bethgali.com

Silvia Vespasiani
E s_vespasiani@telefonica.net

Arola Tous
E arola@bethgali.com

From Texture to Architecture

Garden of Grasses
 Jardins de graminées
 1994

Bob Wilson
131 Varick Street, Room 98
New York
NY 10013-1410
USA
www.robertwilson.com

Mark Rudkin
P.O. Box 29
78320 Le Mesnil Saint Denis
France
T +33 (0)1 34 61 99 09

Jacqueline's Garden
 Un Jardin pour Jacqueline 2001

Eva Demarelatrous
16, rue de la Voie
85450 Puyravault
France
T +33 (0)2 51 28 64 84

Michel and Geneviève Gallais
1 rue des Cordiers
17230 Marans
France
T +33 (0)5 46 01 78 33
or contact the Town Hall:
T +33 (0)5 46 01 16 56
F +33 (0)5 46 01 01 72

Michel Arnaud
4 Place de la Mairie
85450 Sainte Radegonde des
 Noyers
France
T +33 (0)2 51 28 62 44
E arnaudmi@yahoo.fr

3 Outdoor Art

Structures and Sculptures

The Gloriette 1992

Fernando Caruncho
Po del Narcea, 13
Urb. Ciudalcampo
28707 S.S. de los Reyes
Madrid
Spain
E f@fernandocaruncho.com
www.fernandocaruncho.com

Does the Mint Lie ?
 Mente la Menta? 2000

Land-I: Marco Antonini, Roberto
Capecci and Raffaella Sini
Via Massimi 96
00100 Roma
Italy
T +39 (0)6 349 473 0515
E r.capecci@tiscalinet.it

Moving Designs

Nature's Code Code naturel 2000

pep Studio
Katharina Schütze, Uwe Müller
 and Jürgen Stellwag
Fehmarner Strasse 16
13353 Berlin
Germany
T +49 30 453 93 58
F +49 40 360 357 9962
E Pepita229@aol.com

Water Carousel
 Le Carrousel d'Eau 1997

Michèle Elsaïr
25 rue de Hauteville
75010 Paris
France
T +33 (0)1 42 46 35 59
F +33 (0)1 43 49 66 42

Jean-Pierre Delettre
3, rue Pasteur
89110 Chassy
France
T +33 (0)6 75 01 11 68
F +33 (0)3 86 91 54 23
F +33 (0)3 86 91 53 22

E ricbarbier@yahoo.fr

The Sound of Music

Garden Organs
1996–2002

Jean Grelier
Mairie d'Orléans
45040 Orléans
France
T +33 (0)2 38 79 26 60
F +33 (0)2 38 79 20 23

Eric Verrier
T +33 (0)2 38 52 10 79

Bartolomeo Formentelli
T +39 045 770 13 57
F +39 045 680 06 73

Storytelling

From Sky to Earth
1997–99

Fumiako Takano
Takano Landscape Planning Co.,
Nishi 1–37 Mannen Otofuke-cho
Kato-gun
080-0344 Hokkaido
Japan
T +81 (0)155 42 3181
F +81 (0)155 42 3863
E takano@tlp.co.jp
www.tlp.co.jp

Bricks, Bones and Pumpkins
Jardin des os 2000

Adriaan Geuze
West 8 Landscape Architects &
Urban Planners
P.O. Box 24326
3007 DH Rotterdam
The Netherlands
T +31 (0)10 485 58 01
F +31 (0)10 485 63 23
E west8@west8.nl
www.west8.nl

Power Plants 1993

Peter Walker and Partners
739 Allston Way
Berkeley
CA 94710
USA
T +1 510 849 9494
F +1 510 849 9333
www.pwpla.com

Inside Stories

Straw Hut Garden
Jardin de paille
2000

Hugues Peuvergne
42 bis, avenue du Général Leclerc
77400 Lagny-sur-Marne
France
T +33 (0)1 64 30 61 75
F +33 (0)1 60 07 98 04

Woven Willows
Saules tressées 1995–96

David and Judy Drew
41 rue de Jolivet
37190 Villaines Les Rochers
France
T/F +33 (0)2 47 45 25 55

4 Time and Change

Making Time Visible

Mist Garden
Nebelgarten 1996–98

Latz + Partner
Ampertshausen 6
85402 Kranzberg
Germany
T +49 (0)8166 6785 0
F +49 (0)8166 6785 33
E latz.und.partner@t-online.de
www.latzundpartner.de

Nests of the Goddess Mappa
Nids de la déesse Mappa
2002

Remi Duthoit
Atelier HÉMISPHÈRES
26 rue de Bruis
13005 Marseille
France
T/F +33 (0)4 91 47 19 75
E remistral@free.fr

Eric Barbier
3 rue Aude
13100 Aix-en-Provence
France

5 The Landscape Question

Games with Scale

Living Walls
Murs végétaux 1996+

Patrick Blanc
111 rue du Général Leclerc
94000 Créteil
France
T +33 (0)1 42 07 59 95
F +33 (0)1 48 99 86 21

The Pampas: From Monotony
to Infinity Pampa, vers l'infini par
la monotonie 2001–2002

Martina Barzi, Josefina Casares
Estudio Barzi-Casares
El Pueblo
Estancias del Pilar
Panamericana Ramal Pilar, KM 56
1629 Pilar, PBA
Argentina
T +54 11 15 5308 1084
F +54 23 22 402 389
www.barzicasares.com.ar

Symbolic Landscapes

The Earth in Motion
La Terre en marche 1996

George Hargreaves
Hargreaves Associates
2020 17th Street
San Francisco
CA 94103
USA
T +1 415 865 1811
F +1 415 865 1810
E lmitchell@hargreaves.com
www.hargreaves.com

Rhapsody in Blue
Rapsodie en bleu 1994

Jacques Simon
42 rue Delaunay
91240 Saint Michel sur Orge
France
T +33 (0)6 84 11 44 67
F +33 (0)1 64 49 05 15

Context

The Water Triangle
Le Triangle d'eau 1998

Keiichi Tahara
52 rue Bichat
75010 Paris

T +33 (0)1 42 08 80 11
F +33 (0)1 42 06 44 14

Wild Iron Path
Sentier de fers sauvages 1998+

Jean Lautrey
Les Clavelons
04110 Vachères
T +33 (0)4 92 75 64 68
F +33 (0)4 92 75 60 57
E lautreyjean@wanadoo.fr

6 Wit and Whimsy

Contrary Gardens

Nihilium 1995

Vladimir Sitta
Director Room 4.1.3 Pty Ltd.
Level 2, 105 Reservoir Street
Surry Hills NSW 2010
Australia
T +61 (0)2 9211 4130
F +61 (0)2 9211 6057
E room413@tig.com.au
www.room413.com.au

From Moulds to Mould
De la Mosaïculture vers la
moisiculture 2001

Benjamin Avignon
Avignon-Clouet SARL Architecture
88 quai de la Fosse
44100 Nantes
France
T +33 (0)2 40 71 76 40
E benjamin.avignon@libertysurf.fr

Saweta Clouet
3 rue Metzinger
44100 Nantes
France
T/F +33 (0)2 40 69 24 31
T +33 (0)6 72 82 77 58

Cultivated Kitsch

Grandad's Do-It-Yourself Garden
Bidouille de grand-père 1999

Patrick Chappert-Gaujal
41 avenue du Languedoc
11370 La Franqui
France
M +33 (0) 6 80 31 65 74
F +33 (0)4 68 45 71 39
E chappert-gaujal@wanadoo.fr

Eric Martin and Dominique Cazal
59 bis, rue Paul Louis Courier
11100 Narbonne
France
T +33 (0)4 68 65 00 10
F +33 (0)4 68 65 06 07

Topiary for Fun
Topiaires pour rire 2001

Vanucci Piante
Via Vecchia Pratese, 238
51100 Pistoia
Italy
T +39 0573 79701
F +39 0573 735975

Flights of Fancy

Puddle Reflection
Réflexion dans une flaque
d'eau 2001

Serge Mansau
EXERGUE
Studio de création
9 rue de l'Ancienne Mairie
92100 Boulogne
France
T +33 (0)1 48 25 17 69
F +33 (0)1 46 05 55 69
E artplus@serge-mansau-
exergue.com

Green Phantasy Landscape 2002

Grégoire Reynès-Dutertre,
Philippe Dutertre
9 rue des Ecoles
77950 Voisenon
France
T +33 (0)1 64 64 01 74
F +33 (0)1 64 64 01 90
E ph.dutertre@wanadoo.fr
E reynes.dutertre@wanadoo.fr

Arnauld Delacroix
12 résidence Médicis
94150 Rungis
France
T/F +33 (0)1 56 30 91 61
E a.delacroix@mageos.com

Patrick De Bruyn
Le Château d'Eau
12 rue du Val d'Osne
94410 Saint Maurice
France
T +33 (0)1 45 18 12 38
F +33 (0)1 45 18 12 39

bibliography

Albertazzi, Liliana (ed.), *Différentes natures: Visions de l'art contemporain*, catalogue of exhibition at La Défense, Galérie Art 4 and Galérie de l'Esplanade, Paris, 1993

Amidon, Jane, *Radical Landscapes*, London, 2001

Bakhtin, Mikhail, *Rabelais and His World*, Helene Iswolsky (trans.), Cambridge, Mass., and London, 1968

Baridon, Michel, *Les Jardins: paysagistes – jardiniers – poètes*, Paris, 1998

Baudelaire, Charles, 'De L'Essence du rire et généralement du comique dans les arts plastiques', *Oeuvres complètes*, Paris, 1961

Berque, Augustin, *Les Raisons du paysage de la Chine antique aux environnements de synthèse*, Paris, 1995

Brown, Jane, *The Modern Garden*, London, 2000

Charmant, Anne de (ed.), *Art and Design Magazine*, special issue on 'Art and the Garden', no. 57, London, 1997

Clément, Gilles, *Le Jardin en mouvement: de la Vallée au parc André Citroën*, Paris, 1994

—, *Le Jardin planétaire: reconcilier l'homme et la nature*, Paris, 1999

—, *Thomas et le voyageur*, Paris, 1997

Cooper, Guy, and Gordon Taylor, *Gardens for the Future: Gestures against the Wild*, London and New York, 2000

—, *Mirrors of Paradise: The Gardens of Fernando Caruncho*, New York, 2000

—, *Paradise Transformed: The Private Garden for the Twenty-first Century*, New York, 1996

Cooper, Paul, *Living Sculpture*, London, 2001

Corbin, Alain, *L'Homme dans le paysage*, Paris, 2001

Danneyrolles, Jean-Luc, *Un Jardin extraordinaire*, Arles, 2001

Dubost, Françoise, *Les Jardins ordinaires*, Paris, 1984

—, *Vert patrimoine*, Paris, 1994

Francis, Mark, and Randolph T. Jr. Hester (eds), *The Meaning of Gardens*, Cambridge, Mass., 1990

The Garden Book, London, 2000

Goldsworthy, Andy, *Time*, London and New York, 2000

—, *Wall*, London, 1999

Griswold, Mac, and Eleanor Weller, *The Golden Age of American Gardens: Proud Owners, Private Estates 1890–1940*, New York, 1991

Hucliez, Marielle, *Jardins et parcs contemporains*, Paris, 1998

Hunt, John Dixon, *Greater Perfections: The Practice of Garden Theory,* Philadelphia, Pa., 1999, and London, 2000

Irwin, Robert, *Double Diamond 1997–98*, Lyon, 1998 (originally published as 'Change, Inquiry, Qualities, Conditional', *Being and Circumstance*, San Francisco, Calif., 1985)

Jackson, John Brinckerhoff, *Discovering the Vernacular Landscape*, New Haven, Conn., 1984

Jellicoe, Geoffrey and Susan, et al., *The Oxford Companion to Gardens,* Oxford, 1986

Jones, Louisa, *L'Année jardinière de Louisa Jones*, Aix-en-Provence, 1999

—, *L'Esprit nouveau des jardins: un art, un savoir vivre en Provence*, Paris, 1998

—, *The French Country Garden*, Boston, Mass., and London, 2000

—, *Gardens of Provence*, New York and Paris, 1992

—, *Gardens of the French Riviera*, New York and Paris, 1994

—, *Kitchen Gardens of France*, London, 1997

Kienast, Dieter, *Kienast-Gardens*, Basle, 1997

Koraïchi, Rachid, *Portrait de l'artiste à deux voix: entretien avec Nourredine Saadi*, Arles, 1998

Lancaster, Michael, *The New European Landscape*, Oxford, 1994

Lassus, Bernard (ed.), *Hypothèses pour une troisième nature*, Paris, 1992

Leach, Helen, *Cultivating Myths: Fiction, Fact and Fashion in Garden History*, Auckland, 2000

Le Dantec, Jean-Pierre, *Jardins et paysages*, Paris, 1996

—, *Le Sauvage et le régulier: art des jardins et paysagisme en France au XXe siècle*, Paris, 2002

Leenhardt, Jacques (ed.), *Dans les Jardins de Roberto Burle Marx*, Arles, 1994

Maitland, Sara, and Peter Matthews, *Gardens of Illusion: Places of Wit and Enchantment*, London and New York, 2000

Makeieff, Macha, *Poétique du désastre*, Arles, 2001

Meinig, D. W. (ed.), *The Interpretation of Ordinary Landscapes*, New York, 1979

Montero, Marta Iris, *Burle Marx: The Lyrical Landscape*, Berkeley, Calif., and London, 2001

Mosser, Monique, 'Le XXIe siècle sera jardinier', *Le Jardin, notre double*, Paris, 1999, pp. 231–40

Mosser, Monique and Philippe Nys (ed.), *Le Jardin, art et lieu de mémoire*, Vassivière-en-Limousin, 1995

Mosser, Monique and Georges Teyssot (eds), *Histoire des jardins*, Paris, 1991

Ossart, Eric and Arnaud Maurières, *Jardins nomades et tapis de fleurs*, Aix-en-Provence, 1997

—, *Jardins de voyage: 20 leçons de paysage*, Aix-en-Provence, 1999

Page, Russell, *The Education of a Gardener*, Harmondsworth, 1962 (reprint London, 1994)

Péchère, René, *Jardins dessinés: Grammaires des jardins*, Brussels, 1987

Pigeat, Jean-Paul, *Festival de jardins*, Paris, 1995

—, *Les Jardins du futur*, Chaumont-sur-Loire, 2000

—, *Parcs et jardins contemporains*, Paris, 1990

Pigeat, Jean-Paul, and Catherine Dreyfus, *Les Maladies de l'environnement*, Paris, 1970

Pollan, Michael, *Second Nature*, New York, 1991

Potteiger, Matthew and Jamie Purinton, *Landscape Narratives: Design Practices for Telling Stories*, New York, 1998

Profiles in Landscape Architecture, American Society of Landscape Architects, Washington, D.C., 1992

Robinson, William, *Parks and Gardens of Paris*, London, 1878

Roger, Alain (ed.), *La Théorie du paysage en France 1974–1994*, Paris, 1995

Rogers, Elizabeth Barlow, *Landscape Design: A Cultural and Architectural History*, New York, 2002

Rouard, Marguerite and Jacques Simon, *Children's Play Spaces: From Sandbox to Adventure Playground*, Woodstock, N.Y., 1977 (translation of *Spielraum für Kinder*, first published as *Espaces de jeux: de la boîte à sable au terrain d'aventure*, Paris, 1976)

Schama, Simon, *Landscape and Memory*, New York, 1995, and London, 1996

Simon, Jacques, *Tous Azimuts: sur les chemins de la terre, du ciel et du paysage*, 1991

—, *Allées, escaliers, murets: créations de paysagistes européens*, Paris, 1962

—, *Arbres pionniers*, Saint-Michel-sur-Orge, 1976

—, *L'Art de connaître les arbres*, Paris, 1964

—, *Basic design*, Saint-Michel-sur-Orge, 1980

—, *Les Parcs actuels*, Saint-Michel-sur-Orge, 1981

Tiberghien, Gilles A., *Nature, art, paysage*, Arles, 2002

Weilacher, Udo, *Between Landscape Architecture and Land Art*, Basle, Berlin and Boston, Mass., 1996

Wrede, Stuart, and William Howard Adams (eds), *Denatured Visions: Landscape and Culture in the Twentieth Century*, New York, 1991

picture credits

The following abbreviations are used to identify illustrations:
c centre; *l* left; *r* right; *b* below; *t* top

Joëlle Caroline Mayer and Gilles Le Scanff
2–3; 6–10; 13; 16–17;18–19; 19*t*; 20*l*; 23*l*; 27; 28; 29*b*; 30–31; 34; 35*b*; 38–39; 40*b*; 41; 42–43; 44–45; 45*b*; 46; 47; 49*t*; 51; 52; 53; 54–55; 55; 56; 57; 58–63; 65; 66–67; 68–71; 72*c*; 74–75; 81; 83; 85; 90–91; 91*t*; 93*r*; 94*t*; 95; 96; 100; 102; 103*t*; 107; 108–109; 110*t*; 111*b*; 115*l*; 116–17; 118*r*; 133; 136; 137*r*; 141*t*; 143*l*;149*r*; 152–53; 153*t*; 156–57; 160; 161*b*; 166–67; 167*r*; 168; 169*b*; 171*t*; 173; 174*br*; 175; 176; 180; 181*b*; 182–83.

© **Sofia Brignone** 20r; 21; 29*t*; 36; 64; 110*b*; 111*t*; 115*r*; 118*l*; 119; 121; 122; 135*t*; 146; 147*b*; 148; 155; 158–59; 161*t*; 164*r*; 171*b*; 172; 179.

© **Louisa Jones** 40*t*; 48; 49*b*; 50; 72; 73; 94*t*; 104–105; 106–107; 112–113; 132–33; 137*l*; 139;140; 149*l*; 178; 181*t*.

11 Conservatoire international des Parcs et Jardins et du Paysage, Chaumont/Loire; 19*b* Nord Sud Paysages; 22, 23*r*, 24 Lumir Soukup; 25 Frazer McNaughton; 26 Lynden B. Miller, Lynden B. Miller Public Garden Design; 32*t* © B. Marmiroli; 32*b* © Patrick Genty; 33, 35*t* © B. Marmiroli; 37 Blumeninsel Mainau; 45*t*, 66, 76–77 Eric Ossart; 77*t* Claire Gardet, Philippe Nigro; 78 Conservatoire international des Parcs et Jardins et du Paysage, Chaumont/Loire; 79 Claire Gardet, Philippe Nigro; 80 Fernando Caruncho; 82 Land-I Agency; 84 Patrick Chappert-Gaujal; 86–89 pep Studio Berlin; 91*b* Eric Ossart; 92–93 Michèle Elsaïr; 94*b* © Jenny Jones; 97–99 Hugues Peuvergne; 101, 103*b* © Judy and David Drew; 114 R. Hébrard; 120, 123 Takano Landscape Planning; 124–27 Conservatoire international des Parcs et Jardins et du Paysage, Chaumont/Loire; 128 Walker, Johnson and Partners, photography by Dixi Carrillo; 129 Walker, Johnson and Partners, photography by Raymond Rajaonarivelo; 130–31 Hargreaves Associates; 134 Ecole nationale supérieure de la nature et du paysage de Blois, France; 135*b* Eric Ossart; 138*l* Patrick Blanc and Michel Mangematin; 138*r* Conservatoire international des Parcs et Jardins et du Paysage, Chaumont/Loire; 141*b* Barzi-Casares; 142 Conservatoire international des Parcs et Jardins et du Paysage, Chaumont/Loire; 143 Bernard Wolgensinger; 144–45 Hargreaves Associates; 147*t* Jacques Simon; 150–51 Keichi Tahara; 153*b*, 154 Jean Lautrey; 162–63, 164*l*, 165 © Vladimir Sitta; 169*c, t* Bernard Avignon; 170 Michael R. van Gessel; 174*t*, *l* Patrick Chappert-Gaujal; 177 Conservatoire international des Parcs et jardins et du Paysage, Chaumont/Loire.

acknowledgments

Warm thanks to Jean-Paul Pigeat, visionary founder and moving spirit of the Chaumont Garden Festival and the International Conservatoire; to the Conservatoire staff in Paris and at Chaumont, especially Alain Renouf and Erwan Boudard; to the diligent staff at Thames and Hudson where courteous efficiency seems to rule on all levels; to my husband, always my first copy-editor. Thanks especially to Gilles Lescanff and Joëlle Mayer not only for their splendid photography, but also for their help contacting artists.

And warm appreciation to all the designers and architects worldwide who gave generously of their time, information and commentary, including some, like Kathryn Gustafson and Gilles Clément, who have never yet appeared at Chaumont. Rarely has writing a book meant making so many new friends as this one, and for that above all I am thankful.

index